THE MILLION DOLLAR HIGHWAY

Colorado's Most Spectacular Seventy Miles

Written by
Marvin Gregory
and P. David Smith

Photography by
Kathleen Norris Cook

Western
Reflections
INC.

A special thanks to Duane Smith, George Chapman, Pam Larson, Allen Nossaman, Bob York, and Amos Cordova for reading the manuscript; Mary Thompson, Jane Zimmerman, and Katherine Kane for research assistance; Rose Ann Taht, Kathy Swan, Dottie Froese, and Mercedes Penarowski for help with photographs; Jan Smith and Doris Swanson for typing; and Janet Oslund for copy editing.

Published by Western Reflections, Inc.
P.O. Box 1046, Ouray, Colorado 81427

Editor: Jack Swanson
Designer: Christina Watkins
Color Photography: Kathleen Norris Cook
Print Management by Print Net, Alachua, Florida
Printed in Hong Kong

ISBN 1-890437-01-8

CONTENTS

❧ *The Guston mining district included the fabulous Yankee Girl, the Robinson, and the Guston mines.*

🪶 *Nowadays, traffic waits for the snowplows to clean and sand the roadway before starting up the Million Dollar Highway. In the days before the big plows roamed the roads, the old Model T and the natives didn't mind trying it by themselves! (Marvin and Ruth Gregory)*

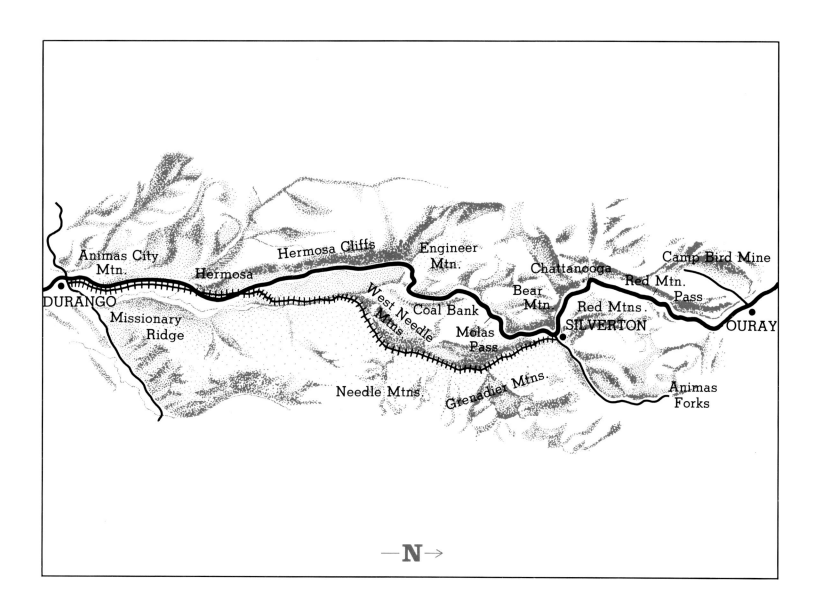

&❧ *The sweeping grace of today's Million Dollar Highway is a far cry from the early-day packtrails and wagon roads which served the region.*

No comparable seventy miles of scenic highway in the state of Colorado offers as much excitement and appeals to such a variety of interests as the Million Dollar Highway. It traverses what many feel is the most primitive, rugged, and beautiful country in all of Colorado. There are deep, shadowy gorges and high mountain passes sprinkled with clear, icy streams, lakes, and waterfalls. The dark green forests of spruce, fir, and pine are liberally mixed with aspens, which can make the mountains glow in the fall when their yellow and orange colors materialize one crisp autumn morning.

The white, snowy summits of the three mountain passes along the route offer far, distant vistas which take in many ''fourteeners''—Colorado's highest mountains. From these vantage points, if one could imagine the world as limited to the visible horizon, it would still seem to be a very big place, indeed. A land of endless mountains is what one climber called southwestern Colorado. The Spanish originally used the name Sierra Madres, or mother mountains, to designate these heights, which can make other ranges seem small in comparison. And scattered throughout, with the stunning natural beauty as a backdrop, are crumbling cabins, abandoned mines, various active mining operations, and some of the most awesome jeep roads in the United States. It is evident that natural forces and human endurance have been in constant battle in the San Juans, and that nature's efforts have often prevailed.

The San Juan Mountains cover approximately 12,000 square miles and are among the newest and, therefore, steepest and most complex in the world. The range has one of the most complete records of geologic forms and features of any mountains in the United States. About twenty layers of rock formations are visible, and, because of folding and faulting, almost two billion years of strata can be seen. The colors of its minerals vary from the dull greys of volcanic ash to the bright reds of the volcanic iron deposits found in the Red Mountains.

Several oceans covered most of southwestern Colorado until about sixty-five million years ago. When they receded, they left behind layers of sediment that were hundreds of feet deep. Later, the central portion of the San Juans rose, and the old sediments were washed to lower elevations, further increasing their thickness. Gradually, those sediments were compressed into massive layers of rock. The lush vegetation along the swampy shores of the oceans eventually became the coal beds of the San Juans. Up to 4,000 feet of the tops of most of the present-day mountains consist of material from volcanoes that existed twenty-four to thirty-four million years ago; but it was the Uncompahgre Uplift, the San Juan Dome (a 10,000-foot rise), and the San Juan Caldera that caused an extensive increase in elevation in the San Juans. Glaciers from three different periods—the Cerro, the Durango, and the Wisconsin —later filled the valleys and covered all but the tallest mountains with what came to be called the San Juan Ice Cap. The deep canyons of the area are largely due to the fact that the last remnants of the glaciers disappeared only 10,000 years ago—yesterday in geological terms. Further erosion by wind, water and chemical reaction then gave the San Juans their unpolished roughness.

Because the mountains are relatively new and the erosion process hasn't had a chance to wear them completely down, the San Juan mountain region is one of the highest areas in the United States: its mean elevation is 10,000 feet. The Continental Divide twists and winds along its eastern edge. More than a hundred peaks are over 13,000 feet high, and fourteen mountains exceed 14,000 feet. (This represents about one-fourth of all the fourteeners in the continental United States.) The San Juans are not a single range of peaks all lined up in a row; they comprise an extensive mountain region. There are many subranges within the San Juans, such as the Sneffels Range, the San Miguel Mountains, and the Needles, which are the most precipitous in the nation and are located at the center of the 10,000-foot-high dome that formed sixty-five million years ago. The different subranges head in every direction, sometimes running into each other and sometimes standing apart from the other mountains altogether. And it was right through the middle of the San Juans that the Million Dollar Highway was eventually built as the major north-south thoroughfare in western Colorado.

All the volcanic activity caused the San Juans to become highly mineralized, with most production eventually occurring in a triangular area formed by present-day Silverton, Ouray, and Telluride. Generally speaking, the ores were produced when the volcanoes fractured the local rock and then magma, mineralized water, and gas solutions were forced from deep in the earth upwards into softer rock, cracks, or crevices. The ore cooled around harder rock into fissure lodes. Replacement deposits also appeared in quartzite and limestone. It is generally true that the higher in elevation or the further away from the center of the volcano that the ore is located, the richer it is because of the cooling process. Wind, water, ice, and chemical breakdown then exposed the ore. And there lay a treasure chest for millions of years until the prospectors came.

Almost 5,000 of the San Juans' 12,000 square miles were eventually incorporated into mining districts. Over one-third of all the gold, silver, zinc, lead, and copper produced in recent times in Colorado has come from the San Juans. Over the years, a billion dollars' worth of metals has been produced, but it was a difficult and trying challenge to wrench them from their hiding places. As costly as it was to find the ore, it was even more expensive to ship, since the San

Juans were so remote, the mountains so steep, and the snow so deep in the winter. Most geologists agree that because of the rugged terrain the rich ores in the area have only been scratched. The majority of the riches await the time when rising metal prices will make it worthwhile to find and remove them from the mountains.

It wasn't just the geography that caused the prospectors problems; the weather gave rise to great hardships also. Because of the wide range of elevations in the San Juans, it is possible for summer to arrive at the lower elevations and five feet of snow to be on the ground thirty miles away near the tops of the high peaks. Every thousand-foot rise in elevation is equivalent, in terms of climate, to driving about 350 miles farther north at sea level.

The San Juan terrain therefore changes through a succession of climates and habitats, the lowest being the rich farming areas in the Animas Valley and north of Ouray. The Upper Sonoran Zone is typified by cottonwoods, willows, box elders, sagebrush, hawks, magpies, rabbits, squirrels, and coyotes, to name a few. It corresponds to those areas at 30 to 40 degrees N. latitude which are at sea level (such as Norfolk, Virginia). The Transition Zone is found between 6,000 and 8,000 feet in elevation and corresponds to those regions at 40 to 50 degrees N. latitude at sea level (as is Portland, Maine). Typical trees and animals of this "foothills" zone include ponderosa pines, junipers, pinyons, scrub oaks, ravens, skunks, porcupines, and deer. Corresponding to a sea-level location at 50 to 60 degrees N. latitude and lying between 8,000 and 10,000 feet is the Canadian or Montane Zone (lower Hudson Bay). This zone embraces the Douglas firs,

spruce, aspens (or quakies), ponderosa pines, grouse, elk, chipmunks, and beaver, among many other life forms. At the top of the high passes lies the Hudsonian Zone. At 10,000 to 11,500 feet, this zone is the equivalent of 60 to 66 degrees N. latitude at sea level (such as Nome, Alaska) and contains thinner stands of spruce, fir, and bristlecone pine, plus thousands of wildflowers, hawks, marmots, and elk. Timberline in the San Juans is about 11,500 feet, and summer at this elevation can be as short as six weeks. Trees do not generally grow above this altitude. But lichens and low, shrub-type plants are common, as well as ptarmigan, mountain sheep, and marmots. More than 5,000 species of flowers, shrubs and other plants live in this fragile tundra region, including the columbine, Colorado's state flower, whose blue and white blossoms are one to three inches long and stand on stalks up to two feet tall.

Weather plays an important role in the San Juans, where fickle nature seems to know only extremes. Snowfall can exceed four feet in a day, and avalanches roar down the mountains; when it warms, and especially during late summer, thunderstorms and floods occur and mud and rock slides abound. The air is clean, fresh, and pure, giving the sky a dark blue color. Those same qualities, however, can cause a person to sunburn easily, and the bright sun in winter can produce snow blindness. At almost any time of the year, the air can be balmy during the day and freeze a man to death hours later. The snow is deep but light, and if the sun is shining the roads can be clear and dry only a few hours after a storm. These same conditions often create extreme danger from snow slides. Over 200 avalanche-related deaths have occurred in the San

Juans in the last century. Today, road crews along the Million Dollar Highway sometimes literally shoot slides down with howitzers or gas-propelled shells in order to control the movement of the snow masses.

Weather in the San Juans is very changeable; sometimes in winter, cloud seeding produces changes; however, the mountains can create their own climate as well. Hot air coming in from the deserts to the west is pushed up by the mountains, and as it cools it drops its meager moisture, causing light rains in summer and dry, fluffy snow in winter. North-facing slopes get less sun and retain more winter snow; therefore, they have more moisture but they are also colder and the vegetation is more like that of a higher elevation. Precipitation increases at about an average of three inches of water annually per thousand feet of elevation gain. Snow can be expected even in the summer at higher altitudes.

Many early-day explorers thought the San Juans impenetrable. John C. Fremont, after nearly dying trying to cross the range, declared them "the highest, most rugged, most impracticable and inaccessible in the Rocky Mountains." Old-timers claim there are only two directions in the San Juans—up and down. But the stormy, dangerous mountains didn't hold back mankind. The lure of the rich minerals drew thousands of prospectors, miners, merchants, and their families into these inhospitable mountains.

The first explorers and prospectors in the area traveled over Indian and game trails, using burros to carry their supplies and to bring out the ore. These long-eared animals were the cheapest and most reliable form of transportation because they were sure-footed and could graze almost anywhere. The patient burro spawned many legends and tales. It was told that unless a burro's ears were tied up while crossing

At one time, David Wood had the largest freight wagon outfit operating in Colorado. His "Magnolia Route" moved forward several times as the D&RG advanced its tracks, since *he freighted from the "end of track" into the San Juan Mountains until the region was totally connected by rails. (Denver Public Library)*

❧ *Looking southward down Mineral Creek Valley toward Silverton, Bear Mountain dominates the skyline.*

a deep stream the animal would drown. In 1879, one animal supposedly went over Engineer Mountain on snowshoes! Another story tells of a burro that fell off the Bear Creek Trail loaded with flour. The weight of the flour turned him upside down, but provided a soft landing for the startled but unhurt beast.

Burros were often used in pack trains, but they could only carry an average of 150 pounds of freight compared to about the 300 pounds which a mule could shoulder. They were not always tied together; sometimes they were driven from behind like sheep. The burro did have one great advantage over the mule, however: it could subsist on sparse browse, and didn't have to be fed hay and grain.

Later, the pack mules came. Horses did not generally have the stamina to work as hard as pack animals, so long trains of fourteen to sixteen mules carried the early-day ore over these mountains. The trails twisted and turned so much that if the mule skinner was alone at the front of the train, he would often tie a bell to the last mule so that he could make sure the animal was still back there. In addition to food for the mines, the mules carried timber, dynamite, and even heavy machinery, such as pieces of mills.

As the mines were developed, slightly bigger trails were needed for wagons. Oxen (usually five yoke to a team) or four to eight horses were used for power. In the San Juans, freight wagon beds were sturdily built because they were used to haul out ore. The Reverend J.J. Gibbons, an early-day Catholic priest in the area, reported traveling the stage over Red Mountain ''in the usual way without any more serious inconvenience than that of being obliged to shovel snow, open the road, and help drag out the horses from the high drifts.'' Average speeds of travel by stage in the San Juans were said to be four or five miles per hour. George Darley, another pioneer preacher of the San Juans, reported that ''traveling in the San Juans, during the years of staging, was not considered a great pleasure by many ... In addition to corduroy, holes, stones, stumps, steep grades and 'muding,' many of the roads were 'sidling' and the curves very sharp, so that four horses were all that could be handled by a stage driver.'' Darley went on to recommend the bronco as the best saddle horse for the mountains because it was ''not too heavy to climb the highest places ... light enough to move down the steep incline with ease and security ... no large horse can stand fatigue, hunger, hardship and abuse so well as the depised bronco .. sold in the west for as low as two dollars and a half.''

Even with good wagon roads, it could still take several days to get from Ouray to Durango. None of the old toll roads between Ouray, Silverton, and Durango were at all suited for automobile traffic, until about 1918 when work was always underway along some stretch of the road. During the long construction period, the project was referred to as ''The Durango-Silverton-Ouray-Highway,'' often shortened to ''D.S.O. Highway.'' Since the federal government had established the ''Good Road Bill'' of 1916 and the Colorado Highway Department was established in 1917, by the early 1920s there were automobile highways being planned and built in many places throughout the San Juans. The estimated number of cars in the state rose from 15,000 in 1916 to 300,000 by 1920. By 1922, automobiles and trucks competed on an equal basis with the San Juan railroads for both passenger and freight service.

With the appearance of the automobile, it was not only easier to maneuver in the mountains, but there was also more freedom for people to travel throughout the United States, thus opening up the tourist industry in the San Juans. The population of Colorado was also booming, going from 25,000 in 1861 to 100,000 in 1876, and jumping to 500,000 by 1900. These factors in turn added to the demand for better roads.

New and gentler grades had to be established for the automobiles; hills and sharp turns had to be overcome as much as possible. For those reasons, many of the old roadways had to be relocated, and the old wagon roads are often still visible in many places, notched into the vertical rock mountainsides. The Million Dollar Highway may not be quite as bad today as the road was in 1883, when Dave Day, a Ouray newspaper editor, described it as "dangerous even to pedestrians ... the grade is four parts vertical and one part perpendicular," but part of the thrill is still the road itself.

A flatlander once asked a local how you get through these mountains. "We don't go through them, we go over them," was the reply. But the Million Dollar Highway itself can now easily be traveled by the average automobile. In fact, the highway is used by several Detroit auto manufacturers to test their new models for mountain performance.

Many of the old wagon roads that were built by the early-day miners to their "diggins" now exist as four-wheel-drive roads, branching off the Million Dollar Highway to forge even higher and deeper into

&❧ *Few pictures exist that show the construction of the Million Dollar Highway. Here, a man is operating a pneumatic drill in preparation for blasting during a widening of the road. When the original road was built, there was no such equipment—all drilling was done with hand steel and a single or double jack. (Colorado Historical Society)*

the surrounding mountains. The old mines and buildings, the equipment and tools, and the old towns and camps still lie forsaken and abandoned all over the San Juans. Many of the old-timers themselves lie buried in the cemeteries of long-forgotten towns they helped to found.

And of those passing over the road for the first time, almost everyone asks, ''How did the Million Dollar Highway get its name?'' Almost always the response has been one of the dozen or so myths or legends that have been around for so long that the teller may actually believe it himself! One story is that the road originally cost a million dollars to build (too high); another, that it would cost a million dollars a mile to build today (too low). Perhaps the most often told untrue version is that the road was surfaced with ''tailings'' containing a million dollars' worth of gold.

The truth about the highway's name is as plausible as any of the untrue versions, but not as romantic. During the reconstruction of a twelve-mile segment of highway from Ouray to the top of Red Mountain Pass between 1921 and 1924, one of the contractors, realizing that the cost (based on accepted bids) would be almost exactly a million dollars, made reference, during a meeting of officials involved with the construction, to ''this million dollar highway that we are building.'' The phrase caught on, and the term ''Million Dollar Highway'' was already in general use when an article in the May, 1923, issue of *Colorado Highways*, the official organ of the Colorado Department of Highways, proclaimed ''This 'Million Dollar Highway' is one of the outstanding achievements of the Colorado Highway Department, the Federal Bureau of Roads and the U.S. Forestry Ser-

Hundreds of varieties of flowers, in almost as many shades of colors, are found in the high country—many above timberline.

vice, all three government agencies having expended thousands of dollars on improvements to the road."

By July of 1924, at the ribbon-cutting and speech-making ceremony near the top of Red Mountain Pass, the road was officially dubbed the "Million Dollar Highway," and a sign was erected to that effect.

On present-day maps, U.S. Highway 550 is usually the only description that appears. Although the name originally applied only to the twelve-mile segment south of Ouray, it is now generally used to describe the entire mountainous portion of the seventy-mile stretch between Ouray and Durango.

The Million Dollar Highway is open year-round, but a few words of caution are in order: in winter, be careful to watch for avalanches. Now that the River-side Slide area is protected by a snow shed, the only avalanche crossing the road that has actually killed people in the recent past is hopefully tamed. But don't stop in the avalanche paths that are well marked alongside the road, and do heed the warnings about chains and snow tires. Also, watch out for snowplows, which are constantly pushing snow off the road during the winter months. Some parts of the highway have been chiseled from the steep mountainsides and have an obvious absence of guardrails. This anomaly is not due to lack of foresight or money, but rather allows snowplows to shove heavy winter snows into the canyons below. At all times of the year, one of the greatest dangers is your fellow traveler, who often crosses the center line or takes dangerous chances such as passing on blind curves. But generally speaking, the Million Dollar Highway, if respected, is usually a lot safer than the freeways of a big city—and it's a lot more magnificent! The breathtakingly

ೀ *There was a good turnout for the dedication of the Million Dollar Highway in July, 1924, a short distance north of Red Mountain Pass. Only days and weeks prior, wagons and stagecoaches were still operating over this road; today, not a horse is in sight! (Colorado Historical Society)*

beautiful trip begins at Durango and ends at Ouray (at least in this book), and we hope that the journey is one you will never forget.

&❧ *Durango, southwestern Colorado's largest city, anchors the southern end of the Million Dollar Highway.*

NARROW-GAUGE BOOM TOWN

The predominance of Spanish names given the geographic features of the San Juans furnishes hard evidence of their early heritage. The Durango area may have been visited by Spanish explorers as early as the 1540s, and many of the early Spanish explorations into the Southwest came by or through the area. The famous Escalante-Dominguez expedition crossed the Animas River only four miles south of present-day Durango on August 8, 1776. The first settlement inhabited by Anglos was a small cluster of cabins located about ten miles north of Durango in 1860, and optimistically named Animas City after the "Rio de las Animas Perdidas," or "River of Lost Souls," which flows near the town. The river, in turn, was named for early Spanish settlers who supposedly drowned while trying to cross its rushing waters.

Many families moved to the fertile Animas Valley in the early 1870s for the purpose of supplying prospectors in the nearby San Juans with hay, grain, and vegetables of all sorts. Generally speaking, the ranchers and farmers did better financially than the miners. Eventually, another settlement (in the northern part of present-day Durango) took the name of Animas City (which has led to considerable confusion with the first Animas City). However, the town couldn't legally incorporate until the Brunot Treaty expelled the Ute Indians from the San Juans in 1874. For some reason, the townsite wasn't surveyed until August or September of 1876, although by then the town already contained some thirty cabins, a few businesses, and a school.

It was officially incorporated on December 24, 1878. Unlike the mountain towns, the lower valley was a good wintering spot, and as a result Animas City had more residents in winter than in summer. By the beginning of 1881, the town reportedly had 451 residents.

The city of Durango was born as the result of the Denver and Rio Grande Railroad's decision to build from Denver into the rich San Juan Mountains. Originally, the D&RG tracks were scheduled to run north and south across the United States, connecting Denver with the Union Pacific on the north and going as far south as Mexico City via Pueblo, Santa Fe, and El Paso. After the Panic of 1873 stopped further expansion of most railroads, the Rio Grande made a detour to the west, reaching Alamosa in 1878. By that time, the riches in the San Juans were evident, and the line continued west, winding in and out of steep canyons and crossing the New Mexico-Colorado border some fourteen times before reaching Durango.

It was the smoke-belching, steam-hissing, little narrow-gauge trains that allowed the railroad to conquer the rugged Colorado mountains; and the Denver and Rio Grande under General William Jackson Palmer led the attack. All the early D&RG lines throughout the state were narrow gauge (three feet between tracks), a fact which gave the company a definite advantage over competing lines, which tried to keep their tracks and equipment the standard four feet, eight-and-a-half inches wide (broad gauge), since they already had thousands of miles of similar track across the plains from the Midwest. Most of the present-day rails on the Durango and Silverton Narrow Gauge Railroad (the line's new name) weigh ninety pounds per yard, but the original narrow-gauge rails weighed as little as thirty. The cheaper locomotives, smaller cars, narrow gauge, and lighter rails all combined to greatly facilitate building through the narrow valleys and rugged mountain terrain that had to be conquered.

The obvious spot for extensive railroad facilities was the Animas City area, but for some reason, now obscured by time, the city's trustees didn't want to cooperate with the railroad. The exact problem is unknown, but was probably a dispute over whether the town would donate a depot or right-of-way. It was a common practice for any railroad to ask the towns along its route to donate facilities because of the commercial stimulation the railroad would bring. Many towns, however, took the position that no favors were due because the railroad would usually reap large profits and the local citizens provided a lot of beneficial business for the railroad.

When Animas City failed to make the necessary concessions, the Denver and Rio Grande decided to build a city to go with its new facilities at a point two miles to the south. Dr. William Bell and Alexander Hunt were asked to select the site for the new town of Durango. Hunt supposedly picked the name because he felt the terrain was very similar to Durango, Mexico, from which he had just returned. The exact meaning of the word "Durango" is unclear, but "Ur-ango" is the Basque word for water town (or a place where travelers would rest), an appropriate designation since Durango became a stopping point for wagon trains, stagecoaches, burro trains, and railroads.

The first stake for the survey of the city of Durango was driven by Charles M. Perin on September 13, 1880, and the mountain to the west of town now bears his name. The new town immediately began to compete with Animas City, and everyone seemed to sense that the railroad would assure its success. By January 1, 1881, over 1,000 people already lived in Durango, even though it wasn't until July 27, 1881, that the Denver and Rio Grande construction train entered the city. The first passenger train arrived on August 1, 1881. The D&RG didn't stop to savor its accomplishments and celebrate with the new town; it immediately continued construction of the line towards Silverton, forty-five rugged and treacherous miles to the north.

Even Silverton, which stood to gain so much by the arrival of the railroad, lost some of its momentum to Durango when John Porter moved the Greene smelter from Silverton to just outside the new city, in large part because of the vast amount of coal that had been discovered in the Durango area. The new town almost overnight became one of the largest cities in Colorado, ranking third in terms of postal transactions before it was even nine months old. There were over 2,000 people living in Durango by January 1, 1882.

Durango was soon to garner yet another honor and an economic benefit when the county seat was moved to Durango from Parrot City after the election in November, 1881. By 1885, Animas City had dwindled to eighty-three residents; Durango boasted 2,254. The new town totally dominated the southern San Juans. The extra boost of being the county seat (and also later the site of a Federal District Court) still adds vitality to the city's economy.

Durango was never a mining town, but rather served as a supply town for the mines, a smelter site, an agricultural community, a wintering spot for the miners from the high country, and a railroad center. The abundance of coal in the area gave one more plus to Durango's economy. The local bituminous coal was especially good for coking, which was needed in the city's smelters.

On July 1, 1889, a tragedy struck which seemed to spell doom for the fledgling town: a fire started in a small, downtown fruit stand and rapidly destroyed seven residential and business blocks in the center of the city. But Durango immediately started rebuilding, and this time, instead of the original hastily erected frame buildings, the town was constructed mainly with brick and stone. Instead of a calamity, the added construction gave Durango even more momentum, and the town continued to boom.

By 1890, the population of the city was over 2,700; and one year later, in December of 1891, Otto

The Durango Smelter, in the southwest corner of the city of Durango, was built on a cape formed by a big loop in the Animas River. The four stacks of what originally was the Greene Smelter are in the background. (Colorado Historical Society)

Mears' Rio Grande Southern had been finished to the west and north, connecting the town via Lizard Head Pass with the Denver & Rio Grande at Ridgway, Colorado. As a result, Durango became an even larger railroad center and the supply and processing hub for the mining towns of Rico, Ophir, and Telluride as well as several coal mining communities that sprang up along the new route. Mears realized the potential of Durango and induced his close friend Dave Day to move his famous *Solid Muldoon* newspaper from Ouray. The paper immediately began to extol Durango's advantages to thousands of subscribers all over the Southwest. Day was always known for being absolutely incorruptible yet overly zealous of any cause in which he believed. His wit was known far and wide but often got him in trouble—it was said that at one time there were forty-seven libel suits pending against him.

Durango continued to flourish as a regional commercial center. Fine homes and hotels were built. Churches, the opera, and other forms of civilization came to town. But at the same time it was acquiring respectability, Durango was a rowdy town and had its full share of saloons and brothels. The area between the river and the railroad tracks became the town's red-light district, and the west side of Main Avenue between 9th and 10th streets boasted many saloons and gambling halls. Some of the bordellos were the 555, the Clipper, the Silver Bell, and a Black establishment called "The Garden of Babylon." (Rumor has it that the latter was destroyed when a disgruntled lover set off a stick of dynamite under it.) The many saloons included the Keg, the Hub, the Gold Room, and the Horseshoe, whose main attraction was a cage full of monkeys. Another saloon's name allowed its customers to truthfully tell their wives that they were at "The Office." Most saloons had games of chance, and the town was full of gamblers like Nutshell Bill, Big Tex, and Beefsteak Mike, all of whom could win or lose fortunes in a single night.

The air and noise pollution of the smelters and the trains competed with the otherwise tranquil and scenic setting enjoyed by the tourists, who were now thronging to Durango. Durango was a stopping point on the Narrow Gauge Circle Tour, an extensive rail excursion through the Colorado mountains. In addition, nearby Mesa Verde and other ancient Anasazi ruins attracted many visitors.

In the late nineteenth century, there was a large push by the white population of Colorado to get the last of the Ute Indians out of their small reservation to the south of Durango. But Indian rights were becoming popular in the United States and the days of simply ignoring previous promises to the Indians were gone. Although Durango's merchants looked upon the Indians as a nuisance, they were quick to welcome them to town whenever they received their allotment money. Besides, the Utes had become another important tourist attraction.

Ultimately, the Indians were allowed to stay but were asked to divide their commonly held land into individual 160-acre parcels. The Southern Ute tribe split over the question of private ownership of land. Chief Ignacio and his band did not want private ownership and moved to the extreme southwestern part of Colorado near Sleeping Ute Mountain, outside of present-day Cortez. There, the Ute Mountain Reservation was eventually founded. After the remaining Southern

ᵇ⸙ *This view is to the northeast across the city of Durango in the 1890s. The flat-topped mesa at the right in the background is the present location of Ft. Lewis College. A large portion of the railroad yards can be seen in the foreground. (Marvin and Ruth Gregory)*

Utes took their choice of land, the rest of the reservation around the present town of Ignacio, some fifteen miles southeast of Durango, was thrown open to the whites. A small scale, Oklahoma-type land rush occurred, but many of the whites were disappointed since the Utes, quite naturally, had taken all of the good land. The land which was not appropriated by either the Indians or the whites was later returned to the Southern Utes to be owned by that tribe as a whole.

Durango's period of rapid growth leveled off in the late nineteenth century when the San Juan mining boom cooled, and with it, the local smelter and coal business. With the decrease in ore and coal shipments, railroading declined. Farming and tourism remained viable, however, and took up the slack that otherwise would have occurred in the local economy. In June, 1906, Mesa Verde National Park was created by President Theodore Roosevelt. Through careful promotion, Durango eventually became the destination area for the new attraction, rather than the town of Mancos, which was much closer to the park. In 1947, what was left of Animas City (now the area around U.S. 550 and 32nd Street) was annexed by Durango. In the middle of the twentieth century, oil was added to the local list of natural resources as large fields were discovered to the south and west of Durango.

The establishment of Fort Lewis College in Durango in 1956 helped the city to grow and provided cultural benefits to the residents. The building of the Purgatory ski area in 1965 and its recent expansion into a major ski resort have helped this growth to continue.

Fort Lewis was established in Pagosa Springs in 1878. It was moved to Animas City in 1880, and later to Hesperus, eight miles west of Durango, where it remained an active military post until it was closed on October 15, 1891. The fort's facilities first became a school for Indians, then a high school, a junior college, and finally a branch of Colorado A&M (now Colorado State University at Ft. Collins). The college is now located on a mesa overlooking Durango and is a four-year school, offering a broad liberal arts program, with a particularly good history department specializing in the history of the Southwest. Because of its original location on Indian land, the college still offers free tuition for all Indian students.

Today, Durango continues to be the major city in southwestern Colorado. This town of over 13,000 persons combines an abundant wealth of climate, location, and natural resources. To the north lie the mighty San Juan Mountains, and to the south is the desert and the historic areas of Aztec, Bandelier National Monument, Chaco Canyon, and Santa Fe. To the west are not only the ancient Indian ruins of Mesa Verde, but also Monument Valley, Canyonlands, Lake Powell, and the Grand Canyon—all within a day's drive.

Many of the early miners who struck it rich in the nearby mountains later came to Durango and constructed fine Victorian homes that are substantially the same now as the day they were built. The town's exclusive residential area was laid out along Third Avenue (originally called "The Boulevard"), and some of the finest homes and churches are still located there.

One outstanding remnant of bygone days is the

Strater Hotel, which is actually two hotels in one—both built by Henry Strater, who was only twenty-one at the time he started construction. The four-story, brick structure on the corner was built in 1888. Strater leased his original structure, but after a disagreement with the tenant, he built the three-story Columbian Hotel next door in 1892. In 1894, the Columbian was temporarily used as an opera house, but the two buildings are now back under one management and are operated as a single hotel.

Of course, the Durango and Silverton Narrow Gauge railroad grounds would probably be the focus of an historian's visit to the city. Besides the engines and rolling stock, the depot and roundhouse are of considerable historical interest since they were built in 1881-1882 and have been well preserved. The little narrow gauge isn't just another lovely antique. The entire railroad has been declared a National Historic and National Engineering Landmark.

Three or four D&SNG trains leave Durango every summer morning, carrying hundreds of sightseers, history buffs, and shutterbugs. The ride, which traverses some of the most scenic country in the world, takes about three-and-a-half hours each way. Reservations are strongly recommended for this popular attraction.

"The train trip into yesterday" packs a million miles of history into forty miles of track, according to country and western singer C.W. McCall. It is one of the most exciting and nostalgic railroad experiences in the United States and has been used in the filming of dozens of movies, including "Across the Wide Missouri," "Butch Cassidy and the Sundance Kid," and "Around the World in 80 Days." It is the only Public Utilities-regulated, one-hundred percent coal-fired, narrow-gauge train still running in the United States. Some of its cars were built as early as 1878, but others are necessarily modern-day reproductions. The locomotives were manufactured in either 1923 or 1925 for the D&RG.

The time is gone when Durango had two railroads serving the town and another branch into Farmington. Those rails have long been severed. Today, the only other section that remains in operation is the Cumbres and Toltec Scenic Railway, which runs from Antonito to Chama.

Although the mining activities in and around Durango have declined significantly over the past one hundred years, the presence of the little train and the many restored houses and businesses make it easy for one to imagine the Durango of yesteryear.

🐾 *An engineer mounts his narrow-gauge iron horse, which will depart Durango and head up the Animas toward Silverton.*

There was no wagon or stage road into Silverton and Baker's Park from the south until 1876, when Joseph W. Wallace, James L. Wightman, and others opened their toll road, which was incorporated that year as The Animas Canon Toll Road Company. It was reported that Wightman had sold his interest in a mine in Summit County, Colorado, for $60,000 and had used the entire proceeds for the construction of the new toll road. Wightman later regained his costs when the Denver and Rio Grande bought the road to use for its right-of-way.

The southern gate of the Wightman Toll Road was located at Baker's Bridge, just south of Rockwood at the head of the Animas Canyon. From Rockwood, the road went up Elbert Creek and through the area now covered by Electra Lake to the top of Cascade Hill. The road then plunged down Little Cascade Creek an amazing eight hundred feet in elevation in a distance of one-and-a-half miles and basically followed the present-day railroad grade up the Animas Canyon, crossing and recrossing the river until it reached the northern toll gate just south of Silverton near the Champion Mine.

On October 31, 1877, Denver's *Rocky Mountain News* reported that the road was nearly finished and that wagons were already traveling over the route, which was a grueling journey, to say the least. The stage coming from Silverton was pulled by two horses until it reached a point ten miles south of Silverton. There, four horses were required to get the coach up Cascade Hill. At the top of the hill, they had to be exchanged for fresh horses. In the winter, it was often necessary to make part of the trip on horseback. At all of the stage stops, there were barns and cabins which could house an occasional overnighter if the weather was bad enough. The toll from Baker's Bridge to Silverton was $6.00 for each passenger.

In 1881, just five years after it was built, the Wightman Toll Road was gobbled up by the Denver and Rio Grande Railroad, which was building into Silverton. After that time, a public wagon road paralleled the D&RG tracks from Durango to Rockwood; from there, the Rico Toll Road could be followed as far as present-day Purgatory; but from that point on, one had to go to Silverton by train or along a narrow, dangerous trail by horseback. Most of the locals didn't object to the lack of a wagon road from the south because it was easier, quicker, and cheaper to take the train. So for almost forty years, the train was to become, in effect, the highway from Silverton to Durango.

For decades the narrow-gauge train carried millions of tons of ore out of the San Juans and millions more pounds of supplies on the return trip. The train became almost the exclusive way to get freight in and out of the Silverton area. What little wagon freight that did make it to Silverton usually went from Del Norte over perilous Stony Pass, which was open for only a short time in the summer. There were other wagon roads, but they were even more dangerous.

When the wagon roads and pack trails were closed for long intervals in the winter, the railroad was the only link that Silverton had with the outside world. The surrounding mountains received a lot of snow, and severe avalanches often blocked the tracks through the Animas Canyon for many days. Because the avalanches carried with them a considerable amount of rock and timber, the railroad could not use mechanized means to clear the tracks. So up to 300 men with snow shovels would manually clear them, sometimes resorting to tunnels when the slides had piled snow fifty to sixty feet high on top of the tracks. Occasionally, the route would be blocked for months; mail and emergency supplies were then taken to Silverton by mules, toboggans, or even on the backs of men on snowshoes.

When the railroad was closed for six weeks in the 1890s, Silverton merchants came very close to completely running out of supplies, and the population was facing certain starvation before the situation was finally relieved. In 1884, the line was

≥ *The D&RG tracks still remain alongside the Animas River in Animas Canyon. The Grenadier Range is in the background. The train is probably a photographer's special used by L. C. McClure when he made the photo. (Denver Public Library)*

obstructed from February 4 to April 17, a period of seventy-three days during which no supplies could be brought into Silverton. The longest closure occurred during an eighty-eight-day period between December 26, 1951, and March 24, 1952. Not only snowslides, but also summer floods caused great problems in this part of the canyon, sometimes washing out miles of track at one time. Severe floods occurred in 1909 and again in 1951, but the most famous one occurred in October of 1911, before winter stocks of fuel and food had been stockpiled by the residents of Silverton. Otto Mears came to the rescue, using every available piece of equipment and employing an average of 235 men per day. It is told that he begged coal from the mines, shops, and even the local residents since the normal supply for the trains in Silverton was soon exhausted. Although he was seventy-one years of age, he supervised the repair for twelve hours a day, seven days a week, and the lines reopened in December before winter set in.

In 1927, when the town was again snowed in, the publishers of *The Denver Post* brought some relief to the suffering population of Silverton: the paper engaged an airplane and a pilot, which flew over Silverton, dropping bundles of the latest issues of *The Post* so that the local people could keep up to date with events in the rest of the world!

Even after automobile roads were built in the 1920s, the extremely harsh winters usually shut the highway down. During the winter of 1923 the only route into town was by railroad from Durango to Needleton, and from there, by pack trains, which were carrying the mail and emergency supplies the rest of the way. One desperate dairyman resorted to sending a ton of hay for his animals into Silverton by parcel post. Regular freight couldn't come into Silverton because the train was stopped, but the mail must go through! The hay was reduced to bundles no longer or heavier than the maximum allowed under postal regulations, tagged, stamped, and sent through at regular rates for a total of $14.00. The government was paying a special rate of fifty cents per pound to get the mail carried in by burro instead of the train, so the postal service lost $986 in the transaction. But the cows had a few more days' supply of hay, and the children of Silverton had milk.

On another occasion, it is told, a mixed (part freight-part passenger) train was cautiously making its way up the Animas Canyon when its path was barred by a giant snowslide. The crew decided to try to back the train out of the canyon, but had proceeded just a short distance when its progress was again halted by another avalanche—one that had come down after the train had passed by earlier. It was obvious that it would require several days to clear the tracks, yet it was impossible for the passengers to walk out of the canyon without snowshoes. The crew banked the fire in the engine to conserve fuel, and coal was carried from the tender to the small, potbellied stoves in the passenger cars. The dining car only had enough food for one round trip, but there was no great cause for worry; some of the train crew broke into one of the freight cars, which was loaded with eggs. For the duration of their wait, the passengers were fed a "varied diet": fried eggs straight up, fried eggs over, soft-boiled eggs, hard-boiled eggs, poached eggs, and scrambled eggs.

Even after the highway was built for automobiles in the 1920s, many Silverton residents would ship their cars by railroad to Durango rather than risk the hazards of the roads. However, the highway traffic slowly began to predominate. The train's existence was in constant jeopardy for many years; but each

Building a railroad through this country came close to accomplishing the impossible.

time it appeared that the Silverton train was doomed, something always happened to prolong its life. The railroad was eventually rediscovered by tourists in the early 1950s. During the period that followed, mile for mile, the Durango to Silverton railroad probably produced more revenue for the D&RG than any other part of its system. Nevertheless, the company was constantly seeking permission to abandon the line. "We're in the freight-hauling business; we don't want to be in the tourist business," was their claim. In 1955, the modern, paved road between Durango and Silverton became a reality and trucks and automobiles became the more common mode of transportation between the two towns. The D&RG abandoned its tracks from Antonito to Durango in the 1960s, thereby isolating the forty-five-mile stretch into Silverton. On March 25, 1981, the line was sold to Charles E. Bradshaw, Jr., who created the Durango and Silverton Narrow Gauge Railroad. The Silverton train survives when all others have failed because it has always been as much tourist as mining oriented. Hundreds of thousands of visitors now find both the railroad and the highway a delightful, breathtaking experience.

Today, the historic tracks closely parallel the Million Dollar Highway for eleven miles north out of Durango up the broad and beautiful Animas Valley. The rails begin to twist out of the valley floor as they reach Rockwood, where the railroad and the Million Dollar Highway part their ways—the railroad entering the Animas Gorge between the Needle and West Needle mountains, and the highway passing between Engineer Mountain and the West Needles.

It was impossible to construct the railroad

through the lower part of the Animas Canyon or to follow the steep grades that the Million Dollar Highway now passes over, so it was necessary, at a spot just north of Rockwood, to enter the spectacular Animas Gorge about halfway up its sheer walls. In 1885, George Crofutt toured the state, writing his *Grip-Sack Guide of Colorado*. He described the next five miles of the route as "apparently impassable for a hummingbird," but the railroad made it. The entrance to the canyon was blasted for 900 feet through solid red granite. At a cost, in 1882, of about $140,000 for one-and-a-quarter miles of track, the shelf road stands as one of the great engineering feats in railroad history. The train almost doubles back on itself as it creeps along the eight-foot-wide ledge some 400 feet above the river. Because of the tight curve, there are permanent orders to go no faster than five miles per hour through this section, and the squealing and groaning of the wheels make the ride even more exciting.

The track slowly lowers itself toward the bottom of the canyon until it follows alongside the boiling river, which it crosses three times. The railroad forges into the remote and primitive Needles Wilderness Area, which is part of the two-million-acre San Juan National Forest. Most of the territory from Rockwood to Silverton is now accessible only by rail, foot, or horseback; and it is likely that the railroad will forever remain the only easy access into the extremely rugged region of natural wilderness which straddles the Continental Divide.

At Tacoma (elevation 7,313 feet), a hydroelectric generating plant was built in 1905, driven by a giant Pelton Wheel and powered by the force of water which

Number 480 sits panting on the streets of Silverton, having just finished its uphill journey.

fell 1,071 feet from nearby Electra Lake. The settlement was a true company town, named by an employee after his hometown in Washington state. The early-day company employees and their families who were required to live there made up the entire population of the place; a post office existed because of them. Access to Tacoma was by rail only; sometimes when no train was running and the need was acute, it was necessary to walk the track three miles to Rockwood, the nearest access to a highway.

Cascade (elevation 7,712 feet) was originally a stage stop and post office at the top of Cascade Hill. The small settlement was started in 1873 and had a post office from 1880 until 1882. When the railroad came, the town at the top of the hill was abandoned, a section house was built near the railroad, and a small settlement, also called Cascade, sprang up at the bottom of the hill. It was at Cascade siding that the railroad eliminated the stage road northwards toward Silverton. In 1885, Crofutt was so enamored with the old Cascade that he gave it more space in his *Grip-Sack Guide of Colorado* than he did Durango. In part, he wrote that it ''consisted of a stage-station, a post office, a hotel, all in one *little lone cabin* on the summit of Cascade Hill, 22 miles south from Silverton; 26 miles north from Durango, and 15 miles east by trail, from Rico. 'Oh it was a dandy, we here got our ''sow-belly'' straight, and a ''shakedown'' on the ground floor.' ''

The next stop on the railroad was Needleton (elevation 8,135 feet). A post office was established May 26, 1882, discontinued for short periods in 1892 and 1896, and closed permanently on January 31, 1910. Needleton was originally a jumping-off point for prospectors but is still used today by backpackers, who follow the miners' old wagon road up Needle Creek east to Chicago Basin amidst the area's fourteeners. The prospectors found a few rich veins in the region, but these proved to be short-lived. Low grade veins still cover the mountains, but it would be much too costly to mine and ship the ore from an area so remote and rugged as this. A little over $200,000 in ore (but worth ten times that much today) was produced from the district before it was almost totally abandoned in 1905.

The Silverton train serves the ''Ah! Wilderness'' guest ranch and the highly rated Tall Timber Resort and makes stops at Needleton and Elk Park for backpackers, fishermen, and hikers to get on and off the train. It is a favorite jumping-off point for people traveling into the Weminuche Wilderness Area. The little locomotives also stop in the Animas Canyon twice northbound and once southbound for water. Several movies have been filmed in the Tall Timber park, and small movie towns have even been built there.

Elk Park (elevation 8,883 feet) was a mining, timber, and cattle camp in the 1880s and 90s. There, a siding and wye allowed the train to turn around and return to Durango if supplies for Silverton were being forwarded by burro or mule trains.

The railroad travels through the Needle range of mountains which spreads out like a giant pinwheel of 13,000- to 14,000-foot peaks. Its name comes from the many steep spikes and horns that make up the range, which actually includes the subranges of the Needles proper, the Grenadiers, and the West Needles. In 1874, Franklin Rhoda of the Hayden Survey was

inspired to write: "In some places the numbers of the pinnacles massed behind one another presented the appearance of church spires, only built after a much grander style of architecture than most of our modern edifices." Some idea of the ruggedness of the area is suggested by the names of a few of its peaks—The Guardian, Knife Point, and Storm King, for example. Windom Peak is the tallest of the Needles at 14,087 feet — just three feet higher than its neighbor, Mount Eolus, which is named for Aeolus, the God of the Winds. Sunlight Peak is the cigar-shaped dome that rounds out the group at 14,059 feet.

The Denver and Rio Grande found the going relatively easy from Elk Park into the gradually broadening valley towards Silverton, and their engineers even made a preliminary survey with a view to extend the railroad to Red Mountain, the rich mining region north of Silverton which was beginning to boom in 1882. The railroad ultimately decided not to build beyond Silverton, however, because the engineers felt the necessary grades would be too difficult. This decision of the D&RG left the door open for "The Pathfinder," Otto Mears, to construct the railroad that the big company thought too difficult.

❧ *Dramatic afternoon thunderstorms are common in the San Juans.*

The beginning of the Durango to Silverton portion of the Million Dollar Highway follows an easy, gentle grade through the Animas Valley; but the magnificent and awe-inspiring conclusion sometimes leaves flatlanders with a death grip on the steering wheel. In fact, as U.S. 550 continues north past Purgatory, the grade remains temperate but twists and turns like a drunken snake. The highway is a journey into the past—not only of man's feeble efforts in the last century, but also of geologic development. As the elevation increases, so, generally, does the age of visible strata, beginning with the youthful, ten-million-year-old bluffs near Durango until ultimately more than two billion years of geologic history have been exposed.

The early-day trail to Silverton closely followed the route of the present road as far as Cascade Creek, where one of the old pack trails went up the creek, around Bear Mountain, and down Mineral Creek. Another route ran up Lime Creek and down Bear Creek. In 1875, a rough wagon road was built between present-day Rockwood and the top of Coal Bank Pass, a distance of sixteen miles. But it was still necessary to use the old Ute Indian pack trails for the additional

fourteen miles into Silverton.

At about the time that the railroad forged its way through the Animas Canyon, a man named Weir built a toll wagon road approximately six miles long from Silverton to Molas Lake (then called Fish Lake), basically following what had been an Indian trail. In 1905, the county bought the Weir road and upgraded and extended it over Coal Bank Hill to what still remained of Wightman's 1876 road. For the first time since 1882, there was a complete wagon route from Durango to Silverton; but it was a terrible road, and the Stony Pass route was still the much-preferred way. In 1909 and 1911, disastrous floods destroyed so much of the wagon road that it became totally useless except for pack animals.

Some idea of just how bad the Silverton to Durango road was, can be gained from the fact that the first automobile to Silverton came in by way of Stony Pass. On August 26, 1910, David L. Mechling, accompanied by John A. McGuire (editor of *Outdoor Life*), brought a thirty-horsepower Croxton-Keeton over the 12,500-foot pass. Although the trip had been planned months in advance in an attempt to get more highways built into the San Juans, it wasn't without its snags: the pair had to build part of the roadway during the journey; the auto had to be pulled part of the way by horses; and the trip took five days from Del Norte. On the way down the pass, people greeted the car every few hundred feet, and when the group reached the Silverton city hall, bells were rung, the band played, and a party was held. Otto Mears was on hand to help promote improved roads for San Juan County and to push for a Durango-to-Grand Junction automobile road. The next day the car made it over Red Mountain to Ouray.

By 1910, serious thought was being given to an automobile highway from Durango to Denver, and two routes were considered—one by way of Alamosa and one by way of Grand Junction. According to the law at that time, two-thirds of all construction money had to come from the counties affected. When Silverton attorney W.N. Searcy and Otto Mears both argued vehemently for a Denver-Grand Junction-Durango highway, and all the counties involved agreed to put up their part of the cost (believing that good roads would help the tourism and commerce of the areas), the state agreed to the route through Grand Junction.

Surveys were made during 1917, and it was determined that the old wagon road between Durango and Silverton could be repaired and elevated to the status of a highway. In July of 1918, work started on the $350,000 upgrading. Progress was slow because of the steep cliffs and because downed trees from the Lime Creek Burn near Molas Pass had fallen, almost forming a barricade; furthermore, thousands of fire-killed spruce were still standing and had to first be removed. Construction was impeded even further by the 1918 influenza epidemic, which hit the San Juans so hard that in Silverton alone, 150 people died in one six-week period. Individual graves couldn't be dug fast enough, so trenches had to be used, one of which contained sixty-two bodies.

The new highway basically followed the previous wagon road, except that it skirted Coal Bank Hill around Potato Mountain to the east through Lime Creek Canyon on what is now known as the Old Lime Creek Road. Bill Compton, Roy Roff, Fred Salfisberg, Bob Lockwood, and one or two others from the Western Colorado Power Company made the first complete trip over the road by automobile in October of 1920, although it wasn't officially opened until later. Planks had to be laid by hand over many of the road's ditches and holes, but the group eventually made it. Except for a modern-day rerouting over (instead of around) Coal Bank, the present highway basically follows the same route as the 1920 road.

Today, leaving Durango, the Million Dollar Highway hugs the base of Animas City Mountain (elevation 8,170 feet) and eventually reveals a view of the Animas Valley. This valley was in great part formed by the Late Wisconsin Glacier, which scoured out the U-shaped canyon with its steep red and brown walls of sandstone that rise hundreds of feet above the valley floor. The old roads from Rockwood to Durango generally followed the eastern and western edges of the valley parallel to the base of the cliffs. There were many ways to get through to the north, and a toll road would have been ineffective, although the project was considered by several men. The present road parallels the railroad.

The low, rounded hills surrounding Durango are

terminal moraines—accumulations of gravel and debris collected by glaciers as they moved down the valley, then left behind when the glaciers gradually retreated. The Animas River further eroded the area, but its action has been minor compared to the glacial action. The river meanders back and forth across the broad and fertile valley without any apparent course because it is following the scoured-out remains left by the glacier rather than a path cut by the river itself. Oxbows and cut-off meanders formed as the river created shorter channels between its narrow, looping bends.

Thanks to the river water, the valley is lush and green in an otherwise semiarid land. Most of the land not currently developed is now used for grazing livestock, and the area has also become a favorite wintering ground for elk, in large part because developers have taken away much of their normal winter range. Although called elk, the animal's name is technically "wapiti." They are larger than deer and weigh about 600 pounds. Their beautiful, large antlers are prized by many a hunter.

On the west, near the middle of the valley, is Waterfall Ranch, obviously named after the waterfall created by Falls Creek as it comes down the steep sides of the valley. The ranch was originally founded by Hugh Lambert and then bought by Thomas H. Wigglesworth, who was the superintendent of the construction crew for the Denver and Rio Grande when it was pushing towards Silverton.

About six miles north of Durango, Trimble Lane leads about one hundred yards west to the site of Trimble Springs. Indians must have used the hot springs located there for centuries before the white

A winter aerial photo discloses the interesting meanderings of the Animas River through a valley not of its own making. The Animas Valley was carved out by glaciers, making a convenient course for the river, which came into existence at a later date. (Denver Public Library)

❧ *Engineer Pass (reached by four-wheel-drive vehicle) presents one of North America's premier panoramas, with fourteen-thousand-foot peaks in every direction.*

man arrived, but the spot was named for Frank Trimble, who settled on the spot in 1874 and is generally conceded to be the first white man to discover the springs. Trimble used them for his own rheumatism and wounds received in the Civil War and reported a remarkable recovery. Eventually, two springs were developed that furnished 150 to 200 gallons of hot water a minute, varying in temperature from 90 to 126 degrees. A small hotel was built, and the waters were advertised as having "a pronounced curative value." Trimble collected hundreds of testimonials to the spring's curative powers, including the healing of rheumatism and kidney complaints, and the "eradication of the tobacco habit..." It was especially popular with the local miners, who used it to combat pneumonia and other hazards of the high mountain areas. Eventually, a large, two-story hotel was built that included fourteen guest rooms. Its grand opening was held on December 28, 1882, and regular excursion trains stopped at the site thereafter because the hotel was within easy walking distance of the tracks.

By 1885, Trimble's population had risen to twenty-six, and by 1900, to fifty. The original frame hotel burned in 1892 and was replaced four years later by a beautiful, forty-room brick building called the "Hermosa House." Eventually, riding stables, a saloon, a bowling alley, a gym, and a large dance hall were all built around the springs. Tennis, golf, and croquet were also offered, as well as hunting, fishing, and hiking. The spot served the surrounding community as a post office from January, 1883, until September, 1900, with only two short interruptions. On July 30, 1931, another fire destroyed the hotel; it was

ᐧᕲ *A 1920s "bulldozer" is shown at work on the Million Dollar Highway. In those days, it would have been called "a team and fresno." It is quite amazing how much earth could be moved—high places cut off, low places filled in—with enough men, teams, and fresnos. (San Juan County Historical Society—Louis Wyman Collection)*

again rebuilt, but this time not to its former grandeur. In 1938, the large bathhouse burned, but by that time Trimble had become a popular dance hall and nightclub. Clark Gable and Marilyn Monroe were a few of the notables who visited Trimble. In 1957, a third fire destroyed the main building, and the area has never reopened. The foundations, pool, and other remains, however, are still visible.

Continuing north on the Million Dollar Highway to the point where the highway crosses the railroad tracks and begins to curve upward into the foothills, one comes to another stagecoach and railroad stop called Hermosa (the Spanish term for beautiful). The area was first settled in 1873, and by July of 1876, a post office had been established. The 1877 population of seventy quickly increased to two hundred by 1880. Hermosa became an important supply town for the farmers and ranchers in the northern Animas Valley.

Pinkerton Hot Springs was located three miles north of Hermosa. The resort was named for Judge J.H. Pinkerton, who arrived in 1875 and was the fifth person to settle in the area. He ran a dairy and ranch; a later owner promoted the springs and named them after Pinkerton. The resort is now a private school, but the hot water bubbles up out of the ground near the west side of U.S. Highway 550. The springs are very similar to those at Trimble but not quite so hot, with a temperature usually in the nineties. Ouray, the famous Ute Indian chief, stopped at Pinkerton only days before his death in 1880 to try to get some relief from his Bright's disease. Evidently, water wells being drilled in the Animas Valley have significantly lowered the pressure of both the Trimble and Pinkerton hot springs.

At the very north end of the Animas Valley, half a mile east of the highway on County Road 250, is the site of Baker's Bridge. A bronze marker erected by the State Historical Society in 1961 commemorates the spot where Charles Baker or his followers built the first bridge in the area. They had left Baker's Park near present-day Silverton in the winter of 1860-61 to start a small settlement in the Animas Valley, where the climate would be less demanding. The bridge itself was 300 feet north of the marker and is no longer standing, but its location is obvious.

Lt. Col. E.H. Bergman, while scouting the area for a site for Ft. Plummer in 1868, came upon the remains of Baker's settlement and reported that "we are astonished to find the signs of civilization and the indications of former presence of white men...scattered profusely in wild and lonely confusion through some 50 half-decayed log houses..." He further reported that the Indians had burned Baker's Bridge and he couldn't cross the Animas. The bridge must have been quickly reconstructed on the same spot, perhaps when Baker returned in 1868 to do more prospecting. Incidentally, Bergman suggested the site of the first Animas City for the fort, but Pagosa Springs evidently won out.

Baker's Bridge was to become a toll station on the first toll road to Silverton and was used for half a century until it was washed away by a flood in 1911. More recently, history was made when Paul Newman and Robert Redford leaped from this spot into the Animas River during a scene from the movie, "Butch Cassidy and the Sundance Kid."

Shortly after U.S. 550 crosses the large bridge over the Silverton Railroad's tracks (a good place from which to view the train), the highway intersects County Road 75. This side road descends into a lovely little park to the east that shelters what is left of the town of Rockwood, at an elevation 7,367 feet. A post office was established in 1878, and after the toll road was finished and the train reached the town in September of 1881, the Rico stage met the train six times weekly. In 1882, the town became the primary work camp for the push through the Animas Canyon, and a wye and siding still exist at the small settlement. The town was named for Thomas Rockwood, who ran the Central (also known as the Centennial) Hotel in Silverton. The stage and the freight business were the mainstays of the local economy.

The Rico House was established slightly north of Rockwood in April, 1880. It served as a hotel and consignment area for freight. At this point, the wagon route forked into two toll roads, the west branch going to Rico and the east branch to Silverton. The Rico road passed through present-day Tamarron, then generally followed the line of the present-day Million Dollar Highway north for about nine miles to the small town of Murnane, near present-day Purgatory at the base of the Hermosa Cliffs. There, the toll road went west

◊ The town of Rockwood is shown here at the height of its boom. The settlement existed mainly as a connection of the stage to Rico with the Denver and Rio Grande Railroad's Silverton branch. The Hermosa Cliffs are in the background. (Denver Public Library)

nine miles to a small settlement named Meserole, in the upper end of Hermosa Park, and then over Scotch Creek Pass seventeen more miles into Rico. The Reverend J.J. Gibbons didn't have many nice words to say about the Rico stage: "Sometimes you traveled in a wagon, at other times in a sleigh, and sometimes you were forced to walk. It was the last straw on the camel's back to have to pay seven dollars for the privilege of riding on the stage."

By 1882, the settlement of Rockwood had a cemetery, school, sawmill, saloon, and a large hotel, among other buildings. There was so much traffic through the town that a blacksmith's shop reportedly stayed open twenty-four hours a day shoeing oxen, horses, and mules. But even after the Rio Grande Southern Railroad reached Rico in 1891 and the stage line was abandoned, Rockwood never failed completely because of the area's quarrying, railroad, and timber activities. The Rockwood area was rich in lime, which was needed at the smelters since Silverton's ore was low in that mineral.

The Forest Service has recognized the importance of the Rico to Rockwood portion of the old wagon toll road (now a National Historic Landmark) by erecting a marker at the Chris Park Campground between Haviland Lake and Tamarron. Traces of the road can be easily seen there, and it now functions as a cross-country ski trail in the winter.

Beyond Rockwood, the Million Dollar Highway parallels the Hermosa Cliffs as far as Tamarron, which is a posh year-round resort. Activities there include golf, tennis, hot tubs, an indoor/outdoor swimming pool, gourmet dining, and even a beginners' ski hill that is lighted for night skiing.

Clouds and the Grenadier Range cast evening reflections upon pristine Molas Lake, doubling the beauty.

Various points along the highway north of Tamarron offer outstanding views of the surrounding peaks. From west to east are Engineer Mountain, Potato Hill (which looks much higher than its 11,871-foot elevation), and the butt end of the West Needle Mountains. At The Needles, the small community located at the point where Elbert Creek crosses Highway 550, one can obtain one of the few good views of the Needle range proper. Pigeon and Turret peaks are the two sharpest peaks, rising almost 6,000 feet straight up. Mt. Eolus is the tallest peak, at 14,086 feet, but almost all the other mountains approach 14,000 feet in altitude.

The Purgatory ski area is located nine miles north of Tamarron. It's a destination resort that includes over thirty-five miles and 630 acres of runs at the ski area proper. In addition to good downhill skiing, there are several kilometers of established track and thousands of additional acres for cross-country skiing, as well as many snowmobile trails. The elevation of the ski area ranges from 8,800 feet at the base to over 10,800 feet at the summit.

The road begins to climb steeply after Purgatory, heading onto the lower slopes of Engineer and Potato mountains. Engineer is the conspicuous, 12,968-foot, pyramid-shaped peak that dominates the view along this stretch of the highway. On the other side of Coal Bank, 13,158-foot Twilight Peak is visible, a prominent part of the West Needle Mountains, which lie between the highway and the Animas Canyon. A legend is told of a fabulously rich gold mine on Twilight Peak that has been lost for a century. At 13,077 feet, Snowden Peak protrudes from the northern end of the West Needles.

An interesting but challenging summer automobile trip is a drive along the Old Lime Creek Road (U.S. Forest Service No. 591), which is basically that part of the early automobile road that skirted Potato Hill to the east and followed the course of Lime Creek. The side road will add half an hour or more to the trip between Durango and Silverton, but it offers good fishing and beautiful views, and a few campsites are available.

The Million Dollar Highway, within a dozen miles after Purgatory, crosses two of its three major passes. The road reaches an elevation of 10,640 feet at Coal Bank Hill, which is actually misnamed, since what looks like coal is in fact shale. In the upper reaches of Coal Creek above the highway is the location of another lost gold mine—the Baker Brothers' Seam assayed at $33,000 per ton at a time when gold was worth $16 per ounce.

Wagons seldom went up Coal Bank—it was only a trail and a bad one at that. In 1877, The Reverend George Darley wrote that "on that part of the trail known as 'Old Coal Bank Hill,' when a long way up, my horse fell while jumping to catch a footing, and rolled more than fifty feet. I was walking behind and came near being carried down with him. The trail was certainly rough."

On the north side of Coal Bank Pass, the Lime Creek Burn is quite evident. An enormous fire in 1879 burned 26,000 acres of the beautiful forest, consuming an estimated 150 million board feet of lumber. Because of strained relations with the Indians at the time, the Utes were blamed; but more than likely, lightning or a white man's campfire was the cause. Because of the high altitude and rough winters, the area would probably still be barren if the Forest Service, the Boy Scouts, and the Colorado Federation of Women's Clubs hadn't started a huge reforestation campaign. Unfortunately, the activities have stopped, even though thousands of acres of replacement trees must be planted before the scarred skeletons of the fire will disappear.

Molas Pass attains an elevation of 10,910 feet. The name is Spanish for "moles," many of which dig in the soft earth surrounding nearby Molas Lake. The Molas Lake recreation area—which includes a campground—is owned by the town of Silverton, but is usually leased to private individuals. The lake lies in a shallow basin dug out by glacial action. In fact, the entire area has been smoothed and scoured by ice, and the scratches, or "glacial striae," can be seen on many of the hard rock surfaces. Nearby, Little Molas and Andrews lakes also offer good camping and fishing, although they are a little harder to get to. Grand Turk Mountain, with its twin summits reaching to 13,087 feet, dominates the skyline to the west, while Sultan Mountain rises to 13,361 feet to the north. The Grenadier Range is visible to the southeast across the Animas Canyon.

Shortly beyond the flat area around Molas, Kendall Mountain (13,451 feet) becomes visible to the northeast across the Animas Valley. It was named for L.B. Kendall, one of the original discoverers and owners of the rich and famous North Star Mine, which ironically lies at the base of Sultan Mountain. Each summer, Kendall Mountain is the site of a most unusual footrace. The runners leave Silverton and climb more than 3,700 feet in elevation before reaching the top of the mountain, then must retrace their route all the way back down to town.

The Million Dollar Highway makes a twisting, narrow descent from Molas and actually passes over the top of some of the area's old mines, including the Champion, Lodore, and North Star, as well as dozens of lesser prospects. Soon the town of Silverton is visible a thousand feet below—so far below that the traveler is bound to question his perspective.

᠊᠊& *Silverton twinkles on the floor of Baker's Park, while above, Kendall Mountain catches the last rays of twilight.*

SILVER BY THE TON

The small town of Silverton, the oldest continuous settlement in the San Juans, is dramatically situated at an elevation of 9,320 feet in the middle of Baker's Park. The narrow, steep-sided valley of about 2,000 acres is approximately one mile wide and three miles long. Baker's Park was formed by glacial scouring and then filled with gravel as the glaciers receded. So massive are the surrounding mountains that Silverton looks like a toy village nestled in the narrow valley. Storm Peak to the north, Sultan Mountain to the southwest, Kendall Peak to the southeast, and Tower Mountain to the northeast all exceed 13,000 feet in altitude. When travel-writer Ernest Ingersoll wrote to his New York paper about his visit to Silverton in 1874, he stated that ''the first question with regard to the San Juan mining district was how to get in, and the second query, how to get out.''

Few towns have survived the hardships that Silverton has had to face. The growing season is just twelve days long; the average mean temperature is only 35.6 degrees; and winter temperatures can often vary as much as sixty degrees in twenty-four hours. Silverton, the county seat of San Juan County, is actually located in the lower half of the county, which itself has an average elevation of 9,400 feet. The cold winters sometimes bring snows that total as much as 300 inches in a year. In the town's early history, such heavy snowfalls often caused total isolation or blockades that lasted for six weeks or more. Even as late as the 1930s, the highways into Silverton were usually closed by Christmas, sometimes remaining closed until the following 4th of July. Today, however, it is unusual for the town to be isolated for more than a day or two at a time, perhaps several times a winter.

The town's name was probably derived from the term ''Silvertown,'' but later, the miners liked the story that it was a shortening of the phrase ''silver by the ton''—the early-day goal of the prospectors in the area. In addition to many other metals, sixty-five million dollars in silver was produced during the period between 1882 and 1918. Over the years Silverton has also been called ''The Silver Queen of Colorado'' and ''The Treasure Chest of the San Juans.'' In 1893, the Sherman Act was repealed, which ended the government purchase of silver, and it looked as if Silverton was doomed; but luckily, large deposits of gold were found soon thereafter.

However, fluctuating metal prices have forced many of the mines in the area to close or change ownership dozens of times.

Spanish prospectors were probably working in the area around Silverton a century or two before the Anglo-Saxons arrived. In August of 1860, Charles Baker made the first recorded appearance when he and six other prospectors came over Cinnamon Pass from the north. He had heard rumors of gold in the San Juans and was looking for a strike in the southern part of Colorado, which Baker hoped would become part of the Confederacy. What came to be known as Baker's Park was still in the middle of Ute territory, and the members of Baker's group said they always kept one eye on the ground and the other looking for Indians. Few signs of gold were found, and the prospectors ignored the silver they uncovered when placer mining the stream beds. The gold was still locked tightly in quartz lode veins in the mountains. However, by October, Baker sent out glowing reports that gold was being found at a rate of twenty-five cents per pan, and because of his Confederate sympathies, he pushed for prospectors to obtain supplies and enter the area from the south, not the north. Other interested parties organized in Denver to join Baker, who was now reporting that the Utes were friendly. On December 14, 1860, S.B. Kellogg, Thomas Pollock, and F.R. Rice began their trip to Baker's Park, leading hundreds of prospectors, including some with families. Several smaller groups also started for the San Juans that winter.

Baker was evidently as much a speculator as a prospector, because he had first laid out the townsite of the early Animas City, organized a mining district, and begun a toll road to Abiquiu in New Mexico Territory. The large group from Denver struggled all winter to reach Animas City by a route through the San Luis Valley in south central Colorado. They left eight to ten families at Animas City (now reported to have twenty-five cabins), built Baker's Bridge, and proceeded to Cascade Creek.

In late March, they camped near a large promontory (now called Castle Rock) south of present-day Purgatory, calling their location Camp Pleasant. In early April, their scouts found Baker already actively prospecting about eight miles north of present-day Silverton. The new arrivals quickly searched the entire Baker's Park area but were unable to locate anything but small amounts of gold. Their hardships were beginning to take their toll, and several people died. By May, some of the group had returned to Animas City and others were on their way back to Denver. The prospectors didn't come close to finding the riches that Baker had spoken of (although he was in fact telling the truth, and rich strikes were later made). After a hearing before a miners' court, Baker was almost hung because of his alleged exaggerations, but supposedly saved himself when he panned gold on the spot and found enough to keep the others looking for more. But most of the men were soon discouraged and left the San Juans by midsummer.

Even Baker and a few other diehards had left by winter since their supplies were exhausted and word had come that the Civil War had started. They struggled out to the south over the then-accepted way into and out of the park—up Mineral Creek to Bear Creek, then over Bear Mountain to Lime Creek and, eventually down the Animas River. Although Baker went directly to New Mexico, several members of his party wintered at Animas City before leaving the area. The San Juans were then forgotten for about a decade, but the stories that the early prospectors told were responsible for later expeditions. Baker returned in 1868, but evidently found nothing worth noting, and left for the winter.

Even though the San Juans were smack in the middle of Ute Indian territory and no great riches had been found, the prospectors still returned. In 1870, Adnah French, Dempsey Reese, Miles T. Johnson, C.E. Cooley, and others combed the mountains for lode veins, staked several claims, and took many specimens to Santa Fe to be assayed that winter. The samples were found to be quite rich, so Reese and French returned in the spring of 1871 with six others, and discovered the Little Giant Lode in Arrastra Gulch. Late that year they sold their mine to Major E.M. Hamilton, who ordered a mill shipped into the area. Even though the Utes protested the intrusion of the miners, the mill arrived in August of 1872. By July of 1873, the mill was producing and the Little Giant had become one of the best known mines in the area. The Utes kept constant pressure on the three or four hundred whites that were now in the area. No incidents occurred, but the Indians demanded that the United States remove the whites. The miners, therefore, erected no permanent structures and lived in tents and brush dwellings. Eventually, troops were sent to keep the miners out of the Utes' land, but the whites insisted that their government should make a treaty and get the Indians out of the San Juans. This was accomplished by the Brunot Treaty of 1873,

although it was early 1874 before it was officially ratified.

With the Utes gone, there was a rush of prospectors into the San Juans. Most came in over Stony Pass and down Cunningham Gulch to Howardsville, at the upper end of Baker's Park. Silverton was built in the broader expanse of the valley to the south, while Eureka, Animas Forks (not to be confused with Animas City), and Mineral Point were built north of Howardsville all the way up the Animas. By 1873, more than 1,500 mining claims had been staked, but all the riches being discovered would be useless unless decent roads could be built to get supplies into Baker's Park and to haul the ore out.

The town of Silverton was platted in June of 1874, and early on, lots were given away to encourage settlement. The original county seat was at Howardsville, but later that year the entire contents of the old courthouse were "pirated" one night and physically moved to Silverton, creating a new county seat.

Silverton also encouraged mills and smelters to come to the southern part of Baker's Park. The Greene smelter was Silverton's first and was built in 1874 by John A. Porter for Judge George Greene. Its components were hauled by burros from Colorado Springs to Del Norte and then over Stony Pass at a reported freight rate of twenty-five cents per pound. The Greene smelter could process twelve tons of ore per day but ran only sporadically until 1879, when it was moved to Durango.

The population of Silverton rose from about fifty in 1874 to around one hundred in 1875. The first post office opened February 1, 1875, but for several weeks

Looking south across Silverton to Sultan Mountain about 1900, it is obvious that Silverton still had plenty of room to grow before using up the available space in broad, level Baker's Park. (Denver Public Library)

the postmaster had to keep the mail in his pockets as he cruised town, for there was no actual building yet available for postal operations. Winter mail in 1875 and 1876 came from Del Norte by snowshoes or skis. By the summer of 1876, there was no doubt that Silverton had established itself over Howardsville as the commercial center of Baker's Park, since its population had soared to well over 500.

In 1875, the San Juan road system finally started to develop when Otto Mears built a road from Silverton to Animas Forks, and a barely passable wagon road was constructed over Stony Pass. Cinnamon Pass was originally an Indian trail but had been crossed in 1874 by the Hayden Survey. Their responsibilities included finding new routes into Baker's Park, but they declared Cinnamon Pass impractical. In spite of their recommendation, a wagon road from Lake City over Cinnamon Pass was completed in 1877 by Enos Hotchkiss, but it proved too high at 13,009 feet, and Lake City itself was too remote for the road to be used much. It still served to lower freight rates from the original $60-per-ton rate to about $40 by 1878.

In 1879 a wagon toll road from Del Norte was completed over 12,594-foot Stony Pass just a mile north of the old route. This dropped freight prices to about $30 per ton from the former $60 rate. Freighters claimed that the earlier trail was so rough that "every ten feet there was a stone projecting from six to eighteen inches, and frequently on the opposite side a hole from six to eighteen inches deep with a tree stump in the middle." The old road had been so bad, there was one steep stretch that couldn't be negotiated with normal wagon brakes. Freighters would cut down a tree and drag it behind their wagon, but

since the spot was near timberline, all the trees were soon gone. One enterprising man secured a snubbing rope to a tree stump and charged $2.50 per wagon (a day's wages) for lowering wagons two hundred feet down that portion of the trail.

In 1879, a wagon road was completed eight miles up Cement Creek to Gladstone and extended to the head of Poughkeepsie Gulch, where pack trails led north to Ouray. There was also a road up Mineral Creek as far as the Chattanooga area, which in 1884 was extended to Red Mountain, where the same year a road was completed from Ouray.

However, Silverton was still often isolated in the winter when the snow piled deep and avalanches sometimes buried the roads under fifty feet of snow and debris. Sometimes the mail just piled up because no one would venture in or out. Even water was sold from sleds in the winter for fifty cents per five-gallon bucket.

When the spring of 1882 arrived, the D&RG was working feverishly along the line north of Rockwood toward Silverton. The Silverton papers carried progress reports almost weekly, and plans for the annual 4th of July celebration included the arrival of the first train. The *San Juan Herald* of July 1, 1882, reported that the first sound of a locomotive whistle had been heard in town, but that the end of the track was still three-and-a-half miles down the Animas River. To the disappointment of the locals, the first train steamed into Silverton on July 8, 1882, four days late for the planned celebration!

When the Denver and Rio Grande arrived, freight rates fell to $12 per ton and passengers could ride all the way to Denver without changing trains, although it took almost thirty hours. Silverton prospered as the supply area for the San Juans, and Durango also benefited from shipping coal and receiving ore for its smelters. In 1887, Otto Mears began constructing the Silverton Railroad over Red Mountain to Ironton, completing the final section in 1888. He also built the Silverton Northern thirteen miles up the Animas to Eureka and Animas Forks between 1895 and 1904. The Silverton, Gladstone and Northerly was built eight miles up Cement Creek in 1899 by the owners of the Gold King Mine. Narrow-gauge railroad enthusiasts have always had a special place in their hearts for Silverton, since four of those railroads entered the town during the last part of the nineteenth century, and three of them made Silverton their headquarters.

The life of Otto Mears, "The Pathfinder of the San Juans," was a Horatio Alger story come true. He was born in Russia in 1840, but both his parents had died by the time he was four years old, and he was sent to San Francisco at age fifteen. Mears joined the Union forces during the Civil War, and after the war worked and traveled in southern Colorado and northern New Mexico. He eventually erected a general store, a sawmill, and a flour mill before building his first toll road over Poncha Pass in 1870 to transport his flour to California Gulch. During the next twenty-five years, he established toll roads and railroads all over southwestern Colorado.

Mears' Silverton Railroad ran a total of eighteen miles over Red Mountain. The Silverton was a promoter's dream, and although it cost $725,000 to build, during its early history it was extremely profitable. Two trains ran twice a day, and a flat twenty cents per passenger mile was charged for the ride. Armed guards rode the ore trains to the smelters in Durango.

Mears promoted his train in a number of ingenious ways. The famous early-day photographer, William H. Jackson, was hired to take pictures of the railroad. Numerous railroad companies issued free passes; however, Mears fabricated his passes from silver or buckskin, and later, even a few from gold. Mears even put the luxurious *Animas Forks,* which was a combination sleeping, dining, and club car, on his train, though the entire trip took only two hours! The Silverton was abandoned in 1921.

Mears also used the *Animas Forks* on his Silverton Northern Railroad. But one of the train's most amusing sights was a handcar built out of two bicycles for Mrs. Edward Stoiber of the Silver Lake Mine. The handcar could operate at a speed of eight to ten miles per hour. Passengers on a "columbine train" once picked 25,000 of the state's flower for a party in Denver. Dignitaries from all over the United States were invited to ride the Silverton Northern. Although the line cost $600,000 to build, much of the cost was borne by mining companies located along the route. The last part of the track had a very steep grade (seven percent), so only two loaded freight cars could go uphill, and three on the downgrade. The Silverton Northern was abandoned in 1936.

Otto Mears didn't build the Silverton, Gladstone and Northerly, but he leased it in 1910 and eventually bought the railroad at a foreclosure sale in 1915 from the owners of the Gold King Mine. The SG&N was a no-frills line. The Gold King bought back the railroad in 1920, but the line was abandoned in 1937.

❧ *The gilded dome and the big clock of the San Juan County Courthouse are reminiscent of Silverton's days of opulence.*

With so many railroads, Silverton became not only a supply and transportation center, but also an important production area. Over thirty mills and two smelters had been built by the turn of the century. The value of ore mined locally eventually exceeded 200 million dollars, and almost 100 tons of gold and 2,000 tons of silver have been extracted from San Juan County to date. As the fortunes of the mines rose and fell, so did the future of Silverton. Various mines that have been or still are famous include the Buffalo Boy, Old Hundred, and Pride of the West in Cunningham Gulch; the Gold Prince in Animas Forks; the North Star on Sultan Mountain; and the Silver Lake, Mayflower, and Iowa-Tiger.

Some sense of how important mining is to Silverton can be gained from the fact that out of the 405 square miles in San Juan County, over 100 square miles are located in mining claims. Gold and silver were what the early prospectors searched for, but lead, copper, and zinc add just as much value to the local ore production. Mining peaked in the Silverton area between 1900 and 1908, and most of its public buildings were constructed during that time. A brief spurt of activity occurred around World War I and World War II, but declined as soon as peace came and the price of metals fell.

The reopening of the Sunnyside Mine in 1959 brought the town back to life. It took two years to run a tunnel from Gladstone to tap the workings, but the Sunnyside is now the largest gold mine in Colorado and the backbone of the local economy. On June 4, 1978, the Sunnyside nearly experienced a major tragedy. One of its stopes (an area from which ore was being excavated) was drilled too close to the bottom of

Lake Emma. Miraculously, when the lake broke through it was Sunday, and there was no one in the mine. As the lake emptied, a torrent of water flooded the tunnels and washed machinery, timbers, and some good gold ore miles down Cement Creek and the Animas River. It took two years to clean up the mess and put the mine back in production.

Silverton still is, and always has been, a typical Western mining town. A two-block-long section of Blair Street at one time contained a good part of the town's forty saloons and some of the most notorious gambling houses, opium dens, and houses of ill repute in the state of Colorado. It was reported that up to some sixty girls worked in the brothels, which usually were descriptively named for their star performers. For a time, Silverton had no property taxes. All the revenue that the city needed was raised by a $500 annual fee for dance halls and saloons and a $5 per month "fine" charged each of the ladies of the night. The tradition was revived in a slightly different way during Prohibition times, when bootleggers were given regular fines for "disturbing the peace." Wyatt Earp dealt cards in a Silverton saloon for months until he was discovered by his old friend, Bat Masterson, who asked him to return to help clean up Dodge City.

Almost half of Blair Street's original buildings are still standing. The street is the northern terminus of the narrow-gauge train and contains a number of false-fronted shops. Many of the buildings on Greene Street (Silverton's main street) look very much like they did seventy or eighty years ago. Unlike most mining towns, Silverton has never had a major fire, so most of its early-day buildings remain. The most prominent of these is the large (forty rooms), fancy, period hotel originally called the Grand and now called the Grand Imperial Hotel. It was built in 1882-83 as the Thomson Block by W.S. Thomson, a native of London, England, for $60,000. Thomson was the royal perfumer for Queen Victoria and had invested a part of his profits in the Sunnyside Mine.

The hotel was opened on July 1, 1883. Originally, the building's second floor was used as a courthouse. The main floor has always housed at least several businesses, including at one time the town's newspaper, *The Silverton Standard and the Miner*. Originally called *The La Plata Miner*, the paper is Colorado's oldest continuous newspaper located west of the Continental Divide. The hotel's saloon was supposedly the birthplace of the song, "There'll be a Hot Time in the Old Town Tonight," when a woman burst into the bar and yelled what was going to happen if she didn't find her husband. Notables who have stayed or been in the hotel include Lillian Russell, Diamond Jim Brady, Marilyn Monroe, and John F. Kennedy.

In contrast to the saloons and bawdy houses, on the eastern slope of Anvil Mountain, overlooking the town, stands a shrine called Christ of the Mines. It was erected in the summer of 1959 by the men of St. Patrick's Catholic Church. The statue itself was carved in Carrera, Italy, weighs twelve tons, and is over twelve feet tall. It is dedicated to the miners of the San Juans. The base and backdrop were made of stones taken from what was once the Fisher Brewery. It was built at a time when the local mining was at a low point in the hopes that it might stimulate that industry. Only months after the shrine was dedicated, metal prices rose and the American Tunnel to the

Sunnyside Mine was started; mining has survived in relatively good shape ever since.

The San Juan County Courthouse on the north end of Greene Street was built out of grey, pressed brick in 1907 at a cost of almost $100,000 (an enormous amount of money for those days), and at the time, it was considered one of the most elegant in the nation. Most of its original furnishings survive intact. The building generally follows a cruciform plan, and its gold leaf dome contains clock faces on four sides.

Behind the courthouse is the two-story brick jail built in 1903, which has housed the San Juan County Historical Society Museum since 1966. The ground floor originally contained an office, kitchen, the sheriff's residence, and a separate cell for women. An office, bath, and the men's cells are still intact on the second floor. The building was used as a jail until the 1920s, when, for a time, it became a home for the indigent. Casey Jones, a Silverton Northern eleven-passenger railbus, is on display outside the museum. It was used from 1918 to 1941 by the Sunnyside Mine and was made from a 1915 Maxwell four-door touring automobile.

Also on Greene Street is the Silverton Town Hall, which was built at a cost of $14,550 in 1908-09 out of red sandstone quarried on South Mineral Creek about three miles west of Silverton. During construction, the four front columns literally fell off and the first contractor was immediately fired. The building has been extensively restored with beautiful woodwork, tiled floors and tin roofs. A circular rotunda with skylights rises for two floors through the interior.

The Carnegie Library was built in 1906 on Reese Street at a cost of $12,000. It was donated by the Andrew Carnegie Library Foundation at a time when the same action was being taken all across the United States. Rev. J. Challen Smith of the Congregational Church secured the grant; the City Council appointed a librarian; and Silverton's residents raised a hundred dollars to buy the books to furnish it. The interior furnishings are mostly original. The basement level was originally designed to be a club room and reading room for men, but now houses the local Historical Society's archives. Silverton, indeed has a rich history to preserve.

❧ *On an ordinary winter's morning at the Silverton depot, the agent has just "parked" his shovel and is now ready to book passengers for the run to Durango—nothing out of the ordinary unless there had been a snowslide in the Animas Canyon. (Colorado Historical Society)*

❧ *At the far end of Chattanooga Valley, Bear Mountain is visible. The bear seems to be licking a honeycomb held in his paw.*

THE RAINBOW ROUTE

It has often been written and believed that Otto Mears built the road from Ouray to Silverton. However, of the several segments of road which were eventually joined together to form one continuous link between the two towns, only that portion from Silverton to Red Mountain Pass and then to the Yankee Girl Mine was built entirely by the famous pioneer road builder. This and other segments of road were finally linked in late 1884 and remained in use, essentially unchanged, for the next forty years.

Some writers have conjured up a vision of Otto Mears building the Million Dollar Highway while standing behind a transit directing the work on his project, but such could scarcely be the case. His many road and railroad projects, for their time, were truly vast undertakings. Although he must have made many on-site inspections, his primary function was performed behind a desk, and his most important tool was his checkbook. While his numerous roads and railroads were of incalculable benefit to the mining regions and cities served by them, and often meant the difference between survival and oblivion, he did not institute those projects out of purely altruistic impulses, but always with a view to profit.

Businessman, promoter, financier, and skillful personnel manager, nothing daunted Mears until the Panic of 1893, when the government ceased to support the price of silver; that eroded the foundations of the transportation empire he had built, and brought it tumbling down around him.

To understand the background of building the road from Silverton to Red Mountain, it is also necessary to explore the history of the road between Ouray and Red Mountain. In 1875, the town of Ouray was founded, but it was extremely remote and there was an immediate outcry for roads to replace the narrow, dangerous packtrails, which were then the only link with the surrounding mines and the outside world. In 1877, a road company was formed to try to connect that town with Silverton and Lake City. After a very inauspicious start, the Ouray, Mineral City, and Animas Forks Toll Road Co. failed. The main road into Ouray became an Otto Mears toll road that ran north from Ouray down the Uncompahgre River to near present-day Montrose and then east to Saguache. The problem was that most of the route went through Ute territory (which was permissible under the treaties that had been made with them).

However, the thought of traveling for many miles through ''savage'' lands bothered most settlers, who kept pushing for a route outside Indian territory. On April 1, 1880, the Ouray and San Juan Wagon Toll Road Company was formed, and road work began that year south out of Ouray toward Silverton. There was progress over the next three years, although it was slow, for finances were always a problem. The initial plan was to build by way of Mineral City to the long-established settlements of Animas Forks, Eureka, Howardsville, and Silverton. A branch road was also planned for the Red Mountain region when, in 1881, rich ore discoveries were made in that district.

By 1882, a boom unparalleled in the history of the San Juans occurred in the Red Mountain district. Consequently, there arose a great cry for roads to the new area. But the Ouray and San Juan Toll Road Company realized that although it had the exclusive rights to build the route, because of its limited funds it could never hope to quickly provide the branch road demanded and still continue the work on what it considered to be the main line to Animas Forks. The proposed road to Red Mountain was therefore relinquished to Ouray County upon the commissioners' guarantee that the road would be built in 1883. The Red Mountain extension diverged from the main road at the Uncompahgre River (Engineer Road) crossing, three-and-a-half miles south of Ouray, and was completed to Ironton that summer. During the third quarter of 1883, Otto Mears stepped in to provide capital, engineers, and an extra work force to complete in three months the lower three-and-a-half-mile portion of the road from the south boundary of the town of Ouray to the Uncompahgre crossing. His fee was high, however— 540 of the initial 1,000 shares, valued at $50 per share, and he therefore obtained control of the toll road.

Silverton in San Juan County, and Ouray in Ouray County, were equidistant from Red Mountain Pass, and each eyed the potential for profitable commerce with the booming, new mining district; thus, they competed mightily to be the first to get roads built into the region. Ouray won the race, even though the terrain was more feasible for a road from Silverton. After having finished the northern portion of the San Juan Wagon Road in September of 1883, Otto Mears was approached by the San Juan county commissioners. They knew that Silverton faced hard times unless they, too, could get to Red Mountain, and they cajoled Mears into building a road from Silverton to the booming area. Mears began building the Silverton-San Juan Toll Road in July, 1884, and with over 350 men working on the road, completed it by November of that same year.

Because Ouray and Silverton had reached opposite ends of Red Mountain, there remained a gap from the town of Ironton to the terminus of Mears' Silverton toll road at the Yankee Girl Mine. Ouray County contracted with Mears to build the last connecting link, and at last there was a continuous road (such as it was) between the towns of Ouray and Silverton. The new wagon road made a much shorter connection than the old pack trail by way of Mineral Point and Animas Forks, which could take a day or two. The new route between the two towns took five to six hours to cover—a distance that can now be traveled in less than one hour by automobile.

Ouray County's actions resulted in seven-and-a-half miles of the road being built with taxpayers' funds; therefore, that section was a public road. Mears, however, controlled access on both ends, so he was able to obtain a higher toll (and the highest profit) from his Red Mountain toll roads than from any of the other routes under his management. The locals complained constantly that they were being taken advantage of, and by 1891, Mears, bowing to pressure, sold the road to Ouray County, reportedly at a price that was less than the initial building cost.

Stagecoach service and a mail route were quickly instituted over the roads that connected Ouray and Silverton, and what was to have been a short branch road became, instead, the main route. The freight rates dropped considerably, and the new road quickly became known statewide for its engineering feats and for the great beauty of the region it traversed. Commerce flowed between Red Mountain, Silverton, and Ouray, but most of the rich ore went out by way of Silverton for several reasons. The road on that side of Red Mountain Pass had southern exposure and was open for longer periods of the year; the Silverton portion had gentler grades because Mears had engineered it with a future railroad in mind; and, at first, the most important consideration was that Silverton already had a railroad connecting it to the outside world. Ore could be shipped cheaply by rail to Durango's smelters, and the arrival of the railroad in Ouray was yet three years away.

When Mears discovered that the team-drawn wagons were so slow and troublesome that they could only carry a fraction of the ore being produced from Red Mountain to Silverton, he began to examine the profitability of putting in a railroad. Eventually, he determined that a railroad could carry 170,000 tons of ore, 1,700 tons of freight, and up to 12,000 passengers a year for gross earnings of over $10 for each mile traveled by the train. This was at a time when most railroads were breaking even at $2 per mile. To further enhance his profit, he evidently overstated the mileage figures of the railroad, with the result that shippers were charged an inflated freight rate. The Silverton train (also known as the Rainbow Route because it curved up toward the sky and down again) took over the path of the former toll road, except at Chattanooga, at the southern base of Red Mountain Pass, where the old wagon road had gone up a series of switchbacks so steep that passengers often had to get out and sometimes even push the wagons so that the teams could make it to the top. The railroad was eventually abandoned in 1922, its right-of-way was deeded to San Juan County and the present Million Dollar Highway was laid out to closely follow the old railroad's bed.

Today, leaving Silverton and heading north towards Ouray, the Million Dollar Highway heads up Mineral Creek Valley toward Red Mountain Pass. The mountains are high and steep, but not precipitous, and they roll back on either side of the valley floor, which in some places is a quarter of a mile wide. The area is one of contrasts: the valleys are carpeted with grasses and low mountain growth, while the fir and spruce on the mountains have been torn aside in areas where avalanches often run.

Just outside of Silverton, across Mineral Creek, are the remains of the North Star Mine and mill. Although in sight of Silverton, the North Star wasn't

ë The old North Star Mill, at the base of Sultan Mountain, stands in ruin amidst fall splendor, just outside of Silverton.

discovered until March of 1879, and it wasn't until extensive work had been done that the owners realized how much their property was worth. It still yields respectable amounts of silver-lead galena.

At almost the same spot on the highway, but in the opposite direction, is an area of jet black, flint-like gravel, which is the residue from the smelting process for refining silver, gold, lead, and copper ores. It was discharged from the furnaces of the Walsh (or Martha Rose) smelter as liquid, white-hot, molten rock and was cooled into a solid mass more closely resembling glass than the original quartzite or siliceous rock. The Martha Rose smelter was built in 1882 and was bought by Thomas F. Walsh in 1894. Walsh later discovered gold in Imogene Basin and developed the great Camp Bird Mine, which made him one of the richest men in the nation.

After passing by the old smelter, the road bears west until it reaches the forks of Mineral Creek and then slowly curves to the north towards Red Mountain Pass. The Silverton Railroad gained elevation more quickly than the present road, and its grade can be seen above the highway for several miles. The South Mineral Creek road, a side road that intersects the highway to the west, is good access to the back country, including a campground that is open in the summer for the many nature lovers, backpackers, and fishermen who congregate here.

About five miles north of this intersection, a sign indicates the turnoff to Ophir Pass, also to the west. This present-day jeep road was a packtrail in the 1870s, but in 1881 was converted to a toll road that became the main mail, stage, and wagon route between Silverton and Ophir. At the time, Ophir was a booming mining camp on Howard's Fork of the San Miguel River. One of the main purposes of the toll road was to carry concentrates to the railroads and smelters at Silverton since it was the nearest access to a railroad. The road is still used as a four-wheel-drive summer shortcut between Silverton and Telluride.

The site where the Ophir Road crosses Mineral Creek was known as Burro Bridge. There were a few cabins in the area—some used as dwellings and others as storehouses or stables for the pack mules and burros that were required to carry the freight over the pass in the winter. The pass lies at 11,700 feet, and large amounts of snow accumulate there.

When Ophir Pass could not be negotiated by horse, mule, or burro, the mail carriers turned to showshoes. They were not required to make the trip during a severe snowstorm, but Sven Nilsen was so dedicated to his job that he refused to wait for one such "flurry" to abate. After all, he had Christmas mail to deliver and felt that it would simply be intolerable for it to arrive late. The risk was great because there are no bigger avalanches than some of those in the wide, deep canyon west of Ophir Pass. Sven buckled shut the waterproof canvas mail sack (which was fitted as a backpack), slipped his arms into the straps, put on his snowshoes, and started out into the howling storm. He failed to arrive in Ophir, nor did he return to Silverton. It was soon suspected that he had been caught in one of those big avalanches. For two years, parties of searchers probed the snow that had been deposited by the avalanches below the trail and watched for signs of the mail carrier, but found nary a clue. Some people began to suspect that Sven had absconded with the mail because it might

🔊 *Only a few pictures of Chattanooga exist. This one shows the town at its peak, with some semblance of streets and blocks. Over forty buildings or tents are visible, many of which were destroyed by a fire in 1892. (Denver Public Library)*

have contained money in lieu of Christmas gifts. Finally, the melting snow, receding from the bottom edge of the large slide, delivered up Nilsen's body, frozen and perfectly preserved, the mail sack still strapped to his back and all the mail dry and in good condition. True to his trust, the mail did reach Ophir, and only two years late!

From Burro Bridge to the foot of Red Mountain Pass proper, many beaver ponds are scattered about the floor of the valley. Beavers live in houses which they build in the middle of such ponds; the houses rise above the level of the water. These large, aquatic rodents leave and enter their houses by an underwater route, but sleep in the upper story above the water. Beavers probably know more about preserving the land, conserving water, reclamation, and restoration than a convention of engineers. They work cheaply and never have cost overruns (and, if given the opportunity, could probably contribute greatly towards the balancing of the federal budget!).

At the end of the Mineral Creek Valley, on the last available spot of level ground before the steep climb up Red Mountain Pass, was the location of the town of Chattanooga. Little evidence remains, but if ghosts were not invisible, they might be observed there as mule skinners, burro punchers, and wagon drivers with their rigs, for these occupations were the reason for the town's existence. Around 1878, entrepreneurs operating in this area furnished supplies to mines such as the Silver Crown, but later, when Chattanooga became a town, it served as a forwarding point for supplies coming from Silverton for the mines in the Red Mountain district. At the peak of the Red Mountain excitement, new mines were being opened almost daily, and new towns appeared every few weeks. Chattanooga itself came into existence in March of 1883 and had its own post office by April 3 of the same year. Most new towns did not grow beyond a small cluster of buildings, but Chattanooga at one time had almost three hundred people and seventy-five buildings, including a hotel, restaurants, and of course the necessary saloons. The coming of Mears' toll road in 1884 hurt the town, and after the arrival of his railroad in 1887 or 1888, there was really no reason for the town to still exist. Certainly, in those days, no one in this town was singing the nostalgic song about the "Chattanooga Choo-Choo." A disastrous fire wiped out much of the settlement in August of 1892, and snowslides destroyed most of the rest. In 1898, Rev. J.J. Gibbons recorded that "ruins of roofs and houses were strewn for half a mile over the valley and the population of this once-flourishing hamlet dwindled down to two" (a saloon keeper and a widow in the laundry business).

There are many snowslides in the Chattanooga area, including the Brooklyn slides to the southeast. They run often, and usually cover the road to a depth that stops traffic until the snowplows arrive. Above Chattanooga to the north are the Telescope and the Eagle which can also be dangerous and can cover the road to a depth of twenty or thirty feet or more.

At Chattanooga the road makes a large bend east to west, coming into the Chattanooga Loop where the highway begins its steep, two-and-a-half-mile climb to Red Mountain's summit. The present loop is almost the same as the large "S" curve that had to be negotiated by the Silverton train, but while the rails and flanged wheels directed the train, the automobile driver must steer hard to starboard coming around the loop. On the curvy ascent, someone in the car (not the driver) might want to watch for the remains of the old Silverton Railroad right-of-way up the mountainside a bit; the not-quite-decomposed wooden ties, their blackened ends pointing toward the highway, seem to be desperately trying to maintain their grip on the mountain, where part of the old roadbed has slipped away beneath them. A passenger (not the driver) might study the view down the Chattanooga Valley in an attempt to discern the image of a bear formed by the trees on Bear Mountain.

A little farther along, a careful observer (not the driver) will note, in a small ravine below the road, the decaying structures of the Silver Ledge Mine, which first operated in 1883 and produced some very valuable ore during its time, although it operated sporadically. The Silver Ledge had a mill at Chattanooga, where the ore could be dumped directly into the cars of the Silverton train. Mills in the nineteenth century charged a penalty for zinc, for that metal had very little market value and was difficult to separate from the other more valuable minerals. A great deal of rich zinc ore was, therefore, left in dumps. Later, in 1904, for the first time, zinc began to be recovered from the Silver Ledge mill in an economically feasible manner.

At the summit of Red Mountain Pass, there is ample room to park the car and let everyone roam about a bit. Topographic maps show the elevation to be 11,075 feet. Here, and everywhere on the Red Mountains, be especially careful around old mining structures. The old buildings are not only private property, but they are dangerous, as well. Many of the mines in the area had shafts that went straight down for hundreds of feet, and many of those shafts are not covered today. A fall into almost any mine shaft would almost certainly be fatal. But stretch your legs, enjoy the scenery, and fantasize a bit about how the place must have appeared back in the days when the Silverton train crossed the summit.

At the top of the pass, switching tracks and a wye had been installed so that the engine could turn around when necessary. Red Mountain Pass, as it is now called, was shown as Summit on the railroad maps. The pass was also known as Sheridan Pass, or Sheridan Junction, after Chattanooga's Jim Sheridan, the local saloon keeper, innkeeper, liveryman, and postmaster. Summit was not really a town; it was simply a place where the railroad's cars could be set on a siding while the locomotive performed its task on the complicated system of tracks in Red Mountain Town and at the mines in the canyons below. No more than two or three cars could be pulled out of the area north of Red Mountain at one time, so round trips were made to Summit to leave loaded cars of ore until the entire consist could be made up for the long, downhill haul to Silverton. With each round trip, the locomotive had to be turned around so that it could take its place at the head of the train.

At the flat spot on the summit of Red Mountain Pass, several old buildings appurtenant to the Longfellow Mine are visible. Here, Otto Mears' old toll road split from the present highway and ran through the Longfellow property, then northeast to Red Mountain Town and down the eastern side of the canyon on the slopes of the Red Mountains to Ironton. At the Longfellow Mine a present-day four-wheel-

&. *The shaft house of the Silver Ledge Mine, a mile from the summit on the south side of Red Mountain Pass, still resists the elements.*

≥ *Intense volcanic action in the area of the Red Mountains left brilliant red deposits of iron oxides.*

drive road leads about a half mile to the southeast to the site of Congress, the earliest settlement on Red Mountain. Congress was at first called Red Mountain City (not to be confused with Red Mountain Town, which is less than a mile to the north). The name was later changed to that of the principal mine in the area. Congress was built in the dead of winter with the foundations of cabins being laid directly upon the hardened snow. It was located in San Juan County several hundred feet south of the Ouray County line and therefore became Silverton's candidate as the best site for development on the Red Mountains. Ouray, on the other hand, backed Red Mountain Town, which was a half mile north, in Ouray County. The editors of papers in their respective towns were always playing up their choice for the Red Mountain settlement and running down the other. Congress' population did rise to about 130 during its prime in 1883, when the mine's production peaked at $220,000, but by 1887, there were only a handful of people still living at the settlement, for the Congress Mine was hardly producing and Red Mountain Town was booming. The Congress Mine was worked off and on between 1881 and 1918 and eventually produced about a half million dollars' worth of minerals from a 350-foot shaft.

Another road leads to the west from the summit of Red Mountain Pass. It is the spectacular four-wheel-drive Black Bear Road that goes over Ingram Pass at 12,840 feet, then past the Black Bear Mine and down the steep mountainside to Telluride. The road is so steep that there used to be a sign at its beginning that stated, ''You don't have to be crazy to drive this road, but it helps.''

Red Mountain Pass is the dividing point separating the watersheds of the Animas and Uncompahgre rivers. The pass is also the boundary line between San Juan and Ouray counties. Northbound, you enter Ouray County as you pass the highest point on the summit.

Many structures in the high country (such as this one at Guston) have never experienced a coat of paint, yet show little decay after the passing of a century.

IMPOSSIBLE DREAM ACCOMPLISHED

From the summit of Red Mountain to the city limits of Ouray lies the twelve-mile portion of road that inspired the name "Million Dollar Highway." Many tales have been told of the section that runs through the Uncompahgre Gorge, such as the story of Ike Stevens, who was traveling with a load of eggs, dead pigs, and two hung-over miners. While crossing a tilting slope, the wagon box came off the runners, shot over the cliff, and came to rest at the bottom of a hundred-foot slope. Ike held tight to the reins and was pulled out of the canyon by the horses, but the miners stayed with the wagon to the bottom. They were fished out sober, alive, but "in an India-rubber condition."

The first automobile came down the Red Mountain wagon road in 1910, but it wasn't until June 22, 1911, that the first motorcar ascended Red Mountain from Ouray. The automobile dealership that sponsored it billed the event as "one of the most remarkable, perilous and daring trips ever undertaken by an automobile on the American continent." The twelve-mile trip took two hours, and a scout was sent in advance on horseback to make sure the way was clear.

Even after the road was upgraded, there were still the large snowfalls and avalanches of winter to contend with; all during the twenties, the route was closed in midwinter. The November 8, 1929, *Ouray Herald* noted that the highway crew had ten tractors and five trucks on hand and planned to keep the highway open all that winter. The Silverton to Durango stretch of road was closed two weeks later, and by January 10, 1930, the Ouray part of the road was shut for the entire winter by the Riverside Slide. It wasn't until 1935 that the road was basically open year-round—closing only in extremely stormy weather for a week or two at a time. Even today with modern heavy equipment, there are periods of time when the road may be closed for two or three days because of high avalanche danger.

Just three-tenths of a mile north of Red Mountain Pass, a narrow, four-wheel-drive road leads a short distance to the east to the site of Red Mountain Town. At the north end of what remains of the town, the walls of the jail are still standing. They are made of 2-x-6 lumber laid flat and fastened with six-inch, cut nails. The jail had two cells but could be quite uncomfortable because it had neither heat nor glass in the windows.

The railroad bed, with its wye for turning the train around, is still plainly discernible. Since the amount of space was so limited, the depot was built inside of the wye and astride the creek, just north of the jail.

The hill to the west of the townsite is known as "The Knob," and on its slope are the remains of the surface structures of the National Belle Mine. The mine was opened in January of 1883 and at first produced easily mined, but not very valuable, soft carbonates, galena, and grey copper. It was in July of 1883 that the big excitement came: an immense treasure cave, filled with pockets of gold, silver, and galena, was discovered. Eventually, the mine was developed to a depth of 450 feet and became one of the largest and best known in the country, reportedly producing over nine million dollars in ore before it closed in 1897.

Red Mountain Town was located in Ouray County on the flanks of Red Mountain No. 3 and was one of two towns vying for permanent possession of the name "Red Mountain" in 1882 and 1883. (The other was Red Mountain City in San Juan County on the south side of the divide.) Red Mountain Town grew to a population of about six hundred; was laid out with named and numbered streets; and had a water system, fire department, and a two-block-long business section on its main street with a full complement of necessary enterprises. There were, proportionate to the town's size, the proper number of gambling houses (including a real estate office), saloons, sporting houses, hotels, and stores marketing such commodities as food, produce and hardware. There were also several fraternal lodges and a miners' union, known as the "Sky City Union." To the east of

The first Silverton train into Red Mountain exchanges passengers with the Circle Route Stage. The end car is a combination passenger and baggage coach. Note the lady in the checked dress and bonnet, standing watch over her luggage. Otto Mears is the fifth from the right. (Denver Public Library)

Main Street was a well-developed residential section.

Rev. J.J. Gibbons wrote that "the lights never went out in the camp, unless when coal oil failed, or a stray cowboy shot up the town. The men worked night and day, shift and shift about, and the people were happy. The gambling halls were never closed, the restaurants did a profitable business, and no one could lay his weary bones on a bed for less than a dollar. Whiskey was as plentiful as the limpid water that gushed from the hills behind the town, sparkling in the sunlight."

Like most Western boom towns, Red Mountain Town was hurriedly built of rough green lumber, and devastating fires were common. In spite of its finely organized fire department, the town burned on August 20, 1892, and again on June 13, 1895. The Silver Panic of 1893 forced a complete shutdown of all silver mining in the state, and very little of the town was rebuilt after the second fire. By 1900, Red Mountain Town's population had dwindled to thirty. That portion of the town that was rebuilt after the 1895 fire was destroyed by a forest fire in 1939.

North of Red Mountain Town and across the valley to the east, on the lower slopes of the Red Mountains, are located many ore dumps and scattered buildings. Actually there are three very red mountains—all in a row. Beginning with the northernmost, they are numbered 1, 2, and 3. They acquired their red, orange, and yellow colors from intensely oxidized surface rocks (the oxides being mainly iron compounds). And scattered across the mountains that Ernest Ingersoll called "gaudier than a cardinal's hat" are the remains of dozens of old mines and derelict mining structures. The right-of-

🐾 *A view of Red Mountain's main street in winter shows the buildings on the east side of the street. There was no means of removing the snow in those days; the best that could be done was to keep a sled track open. (Denver Public Library)*

way of the old Silverton Railroad is still visible among the ruins of the mines.

The camp of Guston was a scant mile below the town of Red Mountain, and although it was not an incorporated town, it nevertheless had its own post office from 1892 to 1898. By 1890, 332 people were living in the area. Eventually, the miners built a small Congregational church which summoned its members to worship by means of both a bell and a steam whistle.

Near the center of the jumble of visible mines is the Guston Mine, from which the entire camp takes its name. The mine was opened in 1882 and developed slowly at first. When the railroad arrived in October of 1888, it became a large producer, eventually reaching a depth of 1,300 feet. It was flanked by two other rich and famous mines—the Robinson and the Yankee Girl.

The Yankee Girl shaft house is the most prominent of the remaining buildings of the Guston camp—a rather tall structure, standing alone, for other portions of the building are now gone. The Yankee Girl was a very rich mine developed to over 1,000 feet in depth and producing some eight million dollars in ore. Ores as rich as 15,000 ounces of silver per ton (almost half the rock being pure silver) were taken from the Robinson, Yankee Girl, and Guston mines. They all closed in 1891, and the Silverton Railroad stopped running past Red Mountain Town in 1898. When the Joker Tunnel was finished in 1907, the railroad briefly reentered that area, but again pulled back to Red Mountain Town in 1912. The Genessee-Vanderbilt Mine was another large mine to the south of the camp. It produced about a million dollars in ore and was worked to 700 feet. Most of the newer buildings on the Red Mountain slopes belong to the Genessee-Vanderbilt, which was operated during World War II.

A mile and a half north of the Red Mountain summit, the Million Dollar Highway winds past the surface buildings at the Idarado Mine. During World War II and for thirty-two years thereafter, the Idarado Mine was one of the largest operations in Colorado, producing great quantities of copper, lead, silver, and gold. Just as the name "Idarado" is a composite of names "Idaho" and "Colorado," so also is the mine itself made up of many parts. Prior to World War II,

the mine was known as the "Treasury Tunnel." That mine itself contained rich veins of copper, lead, zinc, silver, and gold, but the federal government sponsored and subsidized the boring of tunnels to connect several formerly independent but large mines to the Treasury. Eventually, an extensive network was developed, reaching as far as the great Smuggler Mine and the famous Tomboy Mine on the Telluride side of the range.

North from the Idarado, the next two miles of highway twist and writhe, switchback following switchback. This is a good place to spot the yellow-bellied marmot, also called the rockchuck or "whistle pig." These furry, brown relatives of the groundhog are about twenty-five inches long, weigh five to fifteen pounds, and have short, bushy tails. They are vegetarians, but love rubber, often eating the tires or radiator hoses right off a vehicle left unattended in the high country. Marmots hibernate in the winter, but are usually out to bask in the warm sun well before the snow has completely melted in the spring. By fall, they are fat, well-nourished, and ready to spend another winter in suspended animation.

At the lower end of the switchbacks, to the east and just beyond Red Mountain Creek, are a few old buildings of the Joker Tunnel. It was not a mine in the regular sense of the word, but rather a grand scheme to tunnel under the Yankee Girl, Guston, Robinson, and other mines on Red Mountain No. 3. Those mines were all entered by means of a "shaft" (which is vertical) rather than an "adit" (which is horizontal enough to walk along or to accommodate mine cars on rails). The shafts were the most practical means of

🍂 *The shaft house of the Yankee Girl Mine still stands at Guston townsite. What appear to be terraces on the mountainside are actually abandoned roads and the former track bed of the Silverton Railroad.*

mining Red Mountain's silver-copper and silver-lead deposits, most of which were laid down in pipe-like, vertical bodies called "chimneys" or "pipes."

At the time the Joker Tunnel was bored, all the major mines in the Red Mountain district had been worked to great depths. The further down they were mined, the greater became the cost of hoisting the ore to the surface; and of course the deeper they were, the more water that flowed into the shafts, making it necessary to use large pumps so that the miners could work. Both the hoisting and the pumping became so expensive that even with good ore left, there was finally no profit in going further. The purpose of the Joker Tunnel was to drive beneath those mines so that both the water and the ore could be brought out of the tunnel by means of gravity. The ore would then be loaded aboard the cars of the Silverton Railroad, whose tracks were almost at the portal. The tunnel was started in 1905 and was eventually 4,800 feet long. It struck the Guston at a depth of 400 feet, the Yankee Girl at 500 feet, and the Genessee at 600 feet.

The flat but boggy Ironton Park lies to the north of the Joker Tunnel. The valley was carved out by great glaciers during successive ice ages. Later, a landslide partially blocked the north end of the canyon, and Red Mountain Creek and its tributaries then proceeded to build up a thick bed of silt in the valley. In the fall, Ironton Park is probably the best place along the Million Dollar Highway to observe the change in the aspens' colors from spring green to a rich gold sometimes mixed with reds and oranges. The gold color is always in the leaf but is masked by the green of chlorophyll until fall. At that time, a membrane forms at the base of each leaf, which seals off the stem and prepares the tree for the time when its leaves fall. When this happens, the chlorophyll in the leaf disintegrates, exposing the yellow colors. What causes the procedure to begin is still a mystery. The colder nighttime temperatures of autumn may be the reason, but some scientists also believe that the leaves begin to fall off a set number of days after the tree produces its first buds in the spring.

The south end of Ironton Park was the site for the town of Ironton, the settlement from which the park derived its name. In turn, it is said that the town got its name from the iron oxides in the nearby mountains. Today, a few buildings are all that remain of the once-thriving, well-arranged little town, but five days after its birth on March 4, 1883, it already boasted thirty-two cabins. Dave Day reported in *The Solid Muldoon* that "three weeks ago there was not a building to be seen on the spot where Ironton now stands. (Now), over one hundred buildings of various dimensions under headway, and the inevitable dance hall in full blast." By June 1, the booming area was reported to contain ten saloons and two to three hundred cabins. The 1885 Colorado census showed 181 inhabitants, and by 1890, the town reported a population of 323.

But decline soon set in, although Ironton outlasted all other towns in the area—the post office being active until 1920. The town was incorporated and had a water system and an electric light plant. The last full-time residents were the Larson brothers, Harry and Milton. Harry died in the 1940s, leaving Milton behind as the sole resident of the town. Acquaintances soon dubbed Milton the "mayor of Ironton," which led to his winning an expense-paid

🖎 *Ironton's Main Street (which was also the only street) was always busy. Prior to the fall of 1883, freight moving between Ouray and Ironton was carried by pack animal. After the railroad arrived, freight was forwarded from Silverton to Ironton and then on to mines deeper in the mountains. (Colorado Historical Society)*

trip to New York, where he was interviewed on national television about his ''mayorship.'' Milton Larson died in the mid-1960s, leaving Ironton at last without any inhabitants.

North of the townsite of Ironton, a large, high, grey-colored tailings pond fills up a good part of the valley. This fine sand was the result of the action of giant mechanical crushers and ball-mills processing ore from the Idarado Mine. By this means, the metallic elements were released from the rock, and

An autumn snow blankets the ghost town of Ironton.

the tailings were left as waste. Tailings from the Idarado Mine were mixed with water to form a slurry that flowed from the 500-ton mill at the mine through a pipe a distance of three miles to the center of the tailings ponds. Workmen pulled the tailings to the perimeter to form a dike to keep the slurry in the pond until the rest of the tailings settled. The tailings partly cover the old Ironton townsite. The present large mass was deposited over a span of about ten years. After the Idarado mill closed, the ore was hauled out via the Smuggler Portal near Telluride, where it was processed by the company's huge Pandora mill, which was capable of handling 1,800 tons of ore daily.

To the southwest of the big tailings pond is what appears to be a sagging suspension bridge. Two tightly stretched cables, with cross ties bolted to them, supported a pipe that carried the tailings slurry from the mill to the pond. It was designed so that it bowed upwards when it was not loaded, but was level when it was filled.

At the north end of the tailings pond, a jeep road threads its way east into Corkscrew Gulch, leading up above timberline, over a pass at 12,217 feet, and down into the old mining camp of Gladstone. The road was built in 1882-3 for the purpose of connecting Silverton to the Red Mountain mining district by way of Gladstone and Poughkeepsie. Poughkeepsie was described by Crofutt as ''the biggest little mining camp in San Juan Country.'' By 1890, the settlement was abandoned, and little now remains to suggest that a town ever existed.

Near the northwest end of Ironton Park is Crystal Lake, partially enhanced by a man-made dike. Across

This is a view from the Million Dollar Highway looking north toward Ouray. This picture gives a good idea of the immensity of the job of building the first road high on the sides of the canyon. The guardrails were later removed to make snowplowing easier. (Marvin and Ruth Gregory)

the highway to the east are the concrete foundations and a brick chimney of a once-attractive brick lodge that was built in the late 1930s but was destroyed by fire in the early 1950s. An 1,800-foot ski lift was built in conjunction with the lodge. A formal "opening" was held in 1940; guests included the governor and other dignitaries of the Colorado state government. However, some problems arose between the two owners and the lodge was never operated.

A half mile into the deep and awesome Uncompahgre Gorge, three crosses memorialize the Rev. Marvin Hudson and his daughters Amelia and Pauline, and a stone monument has been erected in memory of snowplow drivers Bob Miller and Terry Kishbaugh. All lost their lives to the Riverside Slide, which is located just a thousand feet beyond. A man-made snowshed, the first segment of which was built in 1985, has been erected for the purpose of denying the Riverside Slide any more lives. While any avalanche has the potential to kill, the Riverside was the most deadly avalanche crossing any highway in the state of Colorado because it came 3,200 vertical feet down the mountain, but could not be seen until the moment it reached the highway. In wagon road days, the trail was closer to the bottom of the canyon at the Riverside Slide area, and at times it was necessary to dig a tunnel 600 feet long through the seventy-foot-deep accumulation of snow to allow the stage to get through.

In February of 1897, Jack Bell, who was the mail carrier between Ouray and Red Mountain, was swept off the road and into the canyon by the Riverside Slide. The incident was seen by other horseback riders, and rescue attempts began at once. They probed and dug

frantically, summoning more help and continuing the search until dark. It was finally decided that further efforts would be futile, and all of Jack's friends and acquaintances were reconciled to the belief that he was dead. Twenty-four hours later, Bell extricated himself and had approached within hailing distance of the toll gate at Bear Creek Falls, where he collapsed in the snow. When the tollkeeper saw Jack, he dragged him into the tollhouse, then turned and ran all the way to Ouray to get help. Bell had survived for nearly twenty-four hours under the avalanche and suffered only a small cut and a bruise (although several of his fingers had frozen while clawing his way to freedom and were later amputated).

A half mile further north is the Mother Cline Slide, named for Captain Milton Cline's mine located just above the road. The Mother Cline is usually more dangerous for its ice than for snowslides because in the winter, very large icicles form in this area. The slide only begins 300 feet above the road but runs frequently, stopping traffic.

A mile and a half north of the Riverside Slide, the Uncompahgre River spews out of its canyon from the east and rushes down the mountainside to the bottom of the gorge, not vertical enough to qualify as a waterfall, yet too vertical to merely be called "rapids." Engineer Road follows up the Uncompahgre and eventually provides access to either Lake City or Silverton. This road follows the path of the early-day trail into Ouray. A half dozen ghost towns, dozens of mines, and some of the most spectacular scenery in Colorado are located along this four-wheel-drive road.

The section of highway from the Engineer cutoff

The Mears Toll Road was farther down in the Uncompahgre Canyon and opened in early summer by means of a tunnel under the Riverside Slide. These may be the first freight wagons of the summer of 1888 to attempt the trip to Red Mountain. (Colorado Historical Society)

to Bear Creek Falls was Otto Mears' crowning success, being built an average of 500 feet above the river at a cost of nearly $10,000. At the time, it was one of the greatest achievements ever in road building and engineering in the United States. The Reverend Gibbons reported that "the novice is so alarmed at the sight of the abysses around him that even in the summer, when the roads are good and danger is remote, he alights from the coach and prefers to walk, not trusting himself to the best vehicle and driver."

One more mile and another stream passes under the highway, but barely! Directly beneath the west side of the bridge, the streambed disappears, leaving the water no choice but to plunge 227 feet to the bottom of the chasm, thus creating thunderous Bear Creek Falls. Across the Uncompahgre Gorge is another interesting waterfall called "Horsetail Falls," which, during the early part of the summer or following a heavy rain, trickles hundreds of feet, thread-like, down the bare rocks of the nearly perpendicular mountain wall. At the site of Bear Creek, a large parking area is provided for sightseers who wish to get out of their cars and peer into the gorge below for a clear view of the falls. A monument to Otto Mears was erected just south of the falls in 1926. Bear Creek is a good spot from which to study the area's variety of rock formations, which are partly sedimentary, partly volcanic, and partly metamorphic. Millions of years ago, a 3,000-foot-high glacier ran from this spot all the way north to Ridgway, twelve miles to the north!

Through the tunnel and another mile north is a broad parking area. This scenic overlook affords a marvelous view of the city of Ouray. A big sign there is located almost precisely at the southern boundary of the city, just two "loops and a hurrah" from the beginning of Main Street. The mountains rise so steeply around Ouray that it looks as if there is no escape from the picturesque, little town with its hot springs swimming pool and numerous waterfalls.

&❧ *Ouray glistens after a typical late-day shower.*

GEM OF THE ROCKIES

"The site of the city is one of great beauty, being just inside of the canon of the Uncompahgre River, seven miles from the summit of that name, and consequently on the Pacific slope of the continent, at an altitude of 7,640 feet above sea level. The little park in which it is situated is nearly round, and only about one-fourth of a mile in diameter. On all sides the canon walls and mountains rise, range upon range, peak overshadowing peak, all grooved and furrowed by the hand of the Great Maker, from the tiniest wrinkle to a chasm of gigantic proportions, from the smallest depression and the most rugged ravine to one of the grandest canons in the world. Coupled with this wild scene are cascades, towering pines, leafy shrubs and creeping vines with mosses, ferns and delicate tinted flowers which, with the towering walls, are of every color, shade and hue, sandwiched in, as it were, in the wildest profusion. In the center of this great circle, the grand amphitheater of nature, compared with which, the Coliseum at Rome was an infant, lies the City of Ouray..."

It's difficult to improve upon George Crofutt's description of Ouray, which he wrote over a hundred years ago for his *Grip-Sack Guide of Colorado*. A century has not brought about any noticeable change except where man's influence has been the cause. Crofutt's impression of the size of the mountain park in which the city lies was not quite accurate since the park, from "wall to wall," is actually about one-half mile in diameter; but the horizontal view, as compared with the large vertical cliffs and mountains, does make the park seem smaller. Written about almost any other place in America, his words might seem to be an exaggeration, but applied to Ouray, they may be an understatement.

Although he visited Ouray primarily to gather facts for his book, Crofutt no doubt experienced some of the same excitement that gripped the local populace, and looked in awe upon the mighty mountains that almost demand respect—even reverence.

In the surrounding mountains at the time of Crofutt's visit, mines were employing thousands of workers and were indirectly contributing to the employment of many more in the supporting industries such as transportation, road and trail building, and freighting. There was a seedy side to all this prosperity, however. Ouray boasted a hefty number of saloons and almost a hundred girls working out of cribs and dance halls along Second Street. The Clipper, Bon Ton, Bird Cage, Temple of Music, Gold Belt, and others offered liquor, gambling, sex, and music.

Soon after the town's founding, the word "tourist" became a part of the everyday vocabulary. Word quickly spread about the wonders of Ouray: its spectacular setting; the mild climate (temperatures are seldom extreme, winter or summer); the clear, running streams, cascading waterfalls, beautiful forests, and blossom-covered slopes; the health-giving hot-water springs; and certainly not the least of the wonders, the hard-working but friendly people that populated the place. Here, even a muck-be-grimed miner, just coming off shift, could still manage a wave, a smile, and a warm "howdy."

One example of Ouray's friendliness still occurs at Christmastime—a season when the village already looks like the embodiment of the Christmas dream with its mantle of snow, the church bells that can be heard ringing clear across the town, and the large star and cross situated high on the slopes above the town's blaze of Christmas lights. The local Elks' Club for decades has loaded Santas with bags full of candy and fruit into six or seven jeeps to deliver gifts to every single child (and most senior citizens) in Ouray County on Christmas Eve.

At first, the settlers came to Ouray by whatever means was available: some in wagons, some on horseback, and some even on foot, walking over the many hazardous trails. As soon as there were roads, the stagecoaches did a thriving business, as did several early-day Ouray hotels situated near the ends of the the lines. Early-day sleeping establishments included the famous Dixon House, the Delmonico, and the Sanderson, followed a bit later by the Beaumont, the Western, and the St. Elmo. After the railroad reached Ouray in late 1887, excursion trains frequently brought several hundred tourists a month into the new town.

Although most of the mining towns such as Ouray happily accepted the benefits of tourism, they seldom participated in efforts at promotion, leaving that up to the railroad or to visiting travel writers such as Ingersoll. After all, the main business of the town was extracting silver and gold from the hard quartzite rocks of the San Juan Mountains. In addition to the railroad's promotional activities, many thousands of tourists discovered Ouray on their own.

In 1888, the D&RG inaugurated its famous Circle Tour, which operated in clockwise fashion, covered 1,000 miles, and cost twenty-eight dollars. Technically, the tour started at Pueblo, but it was also possible to take the train from Denver or Colorado Springs. The train followed the southern route via Alamosa, Toltec Gorge, and over Cumbres Pass to Chama, New Mexico. From there, the train proceeded to Durango and then to Silverton, all on the narrow-gauge tracks of the D&RG. The railroad described the journey in its *Tourist's Guide of 1888*: "From Silverton the journey 'Around the Circle' is continued by taking the Silverton Railway...This line does not, as yet, bridge the gap between Silverton and Ouray and from its terminus, stages carry tourists

❧ *In this post-1900 photo of Ouray, you are looking southeast; the D&RG depot and yards are at the lower right. The photograph was taken by L. C. McClure for promotional* *purposes for the Denver and Rio Grande Railroad. (Denver Public Library)*

over the mountains to the latter point where the trip is resumed via the Denver and Rio Grande... The old fashioned stage, with all its romantic associations, is rapidly becoming a thing of the past...Here in the midst of some of the grandest scenery on the continent, the blue sky above and fresh, pure, exhilarating mountain air sending the blood bounding through one's veins, to clamber into a Concord Coach and be whirled along a splendidly constructed road, drawn by four fiery horses, guided and controlled by a typical Western stage driver, is surely a novel and delightful experience.''

The Circle Route then continued through Montrose, Gunnison, over Marshall Pass and back to the place of beginning.

So far as anybody knows, it was in July of 1875 that the first white men set foot in the exquisite, sheltered mountain park where the city of Ouray was to be laid out. Slithering around vertical cliffs and through almost impassable gorges, A.W. "Gus" Begole and John Eckles, who were traveling north in search of mining prospects, suddenly found themselves surrounded by more beauty and grandeur than either of them could ever have imagined. What's more, near the now-famous Box Canyon they discovered strong evidence of rich silver ore! Returning to Howardsville by the same route they had come, they must have taken time to scout, make and mark a trail, for they soon returned with pack burros laden with tools and supplies. They were prepared to spend the winter, building shelters and working their claims. Many other prospectors joined them on their return, and a settlement was quickly established.

On August 11, 1875, Jacob Ohlwiler, John Morrow, and Begole located the Cedar and Clipper lodes between the Uncompahgre River and Second Street, near Box Canyon Falls, although the claim never became a producer. On August 23, A.J. Staley and Logan Whittock discovered the rich Trout and Fisherman lodes, and in October of the same year Begole and Eckles discovered the even richer Mineral Farm Mine about a mile southwest of town. The Mineral Farm was so named because the ore appeared on the surface and the mining was done in shallow, trench-like diggings.

By November, several dozen men had managed to get two wagons of supplies from Saguache across Ute Indian territory. They settled in for the winter, one of them writing home in November, 1875, that Ouray was "as picturesque a little spot as is to be found in America. It is shaped like a bowl, surrounded by high mountains reaching to and above timberline. The only way out is to look up. The sun is a most lazy fellow—always late getting up in the morning, and goes to rest soon after four o'clock at this time of year.'' In December of that year, the first wagon load of ore was shipped out of Ouray to Saguache, although there still was no road to follow. In March of 1876, some thirty newcomers arrived, and by summer hundreds of prospectors were in the area. Again, in 1876, several wagon loads of extremely rich ore were hauled to Pueblo. The long trip took fourteen to sixteen days each way, and only the very richest hand-picked ore would warrant the long and expensive journey.

Soon, a town company had been organized; in 1875, the townsite was surveyed and a plat drawn, and an application was made to the La Plata County

  🍂 *Evening comes to Ouray in segments. The north end of town is shaded by the mountains to the west and will not see the sun again before nine o'clock the next morning.*

Commissioners for incorporation under the name of "Uncompahgre." But the plan failed to materialize, perhaps because of the turmoil taking place in the territorial government as a result of the preparations for statehood by the Territory of Colorado. However, on October 28, 1875, the new settlement was given a post office with the designation of "Ouray." One year later, on October 2, 1876, the new town, now having a population of more than four hundred, was incorporated using that name. The town already had 214 cabins, a school, four stores, an ore sampling works, and the usual number of saloons and gambling houses that always quickly appeared in the new Colorado mining towns.

Ouray's earliest wagon road was incorporated as the Ouray and Lake Fork Wagon Road on November 3, 1876, by Ira G. Munn, Thomas B. Munn, and A.W. Begole. It was intended to link Saguache and Lake City with Ouray, but by spring of 1877 it was evident that the group was not going to complete the project. Otto Mears bought the stock of the company, shortened the length of the road, and finished it almost to the Ute Indian agency (near present-day Colona) by August of that year. In 1878, he completed another road called the Lake Fork and Uncompahgre Toll Road from the Indian agency to the Saguache and Lake City road. Ouray was finally connected to the outside world!

It was reported that in 1878, it cost twenty-five dollars per ton to get ore to the nearest smelter in Silverton, where it then cost twice that much to get the concentrate to civilization. The pack road was often impassable, and because of deep snow the mail didn't come to Ouray until July of that year. Burros and

🙠 The 4th of July parade is "forming up" at Main (Third) Street and Fifth Avenue in Ouray. Most of these buildings still stand. Note the wooden sidewalk across Main Street and the attractiveness of the Beaumont Hotel. (Denver Public Library)

wagons carried freight from Canon City (the nearest railroad) to Ouray at ten cents per pound, and on the return trip transported ore for eighty dollars per ton. The Denver and Rio Grande Railroad reached Montrose in June of 1882, and freight was immediately shipped to and from Ouray at that point. Dave Wood was the main freighter, and Sanderson & Co. ran the stage. In 1887, the D&RG started a branch to Ouray, completing the effort by December of that year. Ouray, first organized as a "town," grew so rapidly that by 1891, it had reached a population of 2,000 and was officially designated a "city of the second class" by the Colorado state government.

With the repeal of the Sherman Silver Purchase Act in 1893, most of Colorado's mining towns began to suffer immediately. However, Ouray was in a better position than many parts of Colorado because Thomas Walsh discovered gold in 1895 at what became the Camp Bird Mine, and rich discoveries were also made on Gold Hill, directly north of Ouray. Ouray's future was thus assured for several decades. The Camp Bird Mine produced over twenty-six million dollars in gold between 1896 and 1910.

Ouray's first structures, of course, had been quickly built of logs or sawed lumber, available because a sawmill had been in operation on the banks of the Uncompahgre River since the first year of the town's existence. Much of the forest that covered the valley floor had to be cleared to make way for streets and buildings, and the timber provided the logs for the mill. The earliest buildings were hastily constructed without the benefit of an architect or engineer, and at first gave Ouray the look of most early-day boom towns—false fronts and simple cabins. It wasn't until 1878 that the stumps were removed and the streets graded.

As the town's prosperity increased, business structures and dwellings of a more attractive and durable design began to appear. Only a few of the earliest log or lumber structures remain standing today, but many of the Victorian homes and other buildings erected during the 1890s and 1900s are still the source of much pride for their owners as well as for the other residents of Ouray.

What is now the excellent Ouray County Historical Museum on the corner of Sixth Avenue and Fifth Street was originally opened as St. Joseph's Hospital in 1887. At one time, it operated under a dues system—those who had one dollar deducted from their paycheck each month would be admitted for free if any emergency made it necessary.

Before the city of Ouray was even ten years old, a brickyard was established which provided brick for the Hartwell building constructed in 1882, and for the public school building which was erected in 1883 and razed in 1939. Most of the buildings along today's Main Street, including the Beaumont Hotel (built in 1886) and Wright's Hall (1888), as well as the Ouray County Courthouse (1888), were constructed of this brick.

Deep pits were created by the excavation of the clay deposits from which the brick was made. Hot water springs in the immediate vicinity, constantly bubbling to the surface in all seasons, filled those pits and created a cluster of little lakes. The lakes maintained a tepid temperature, even in the coldest weather. The owner of one hot spring in another part of town, wishing to make some other use of his spring, transferred a stock of goldfish to the larger ponds at the site of the old brick factory. For years thereafter, the area was referred to as "the fish ponds." The fish prospered, living in those outdoor warm-water ponds throughout the year, needing almost no care or attention, for their food supply also grew in the ponds. In one large remaining pond, near the present-day swimming pool, goldfish still delight children and are descended from the initial stock introduced almost ninety years ago.

In 1921, a two-foot alligator was brought here from Louisiana to live in the ponds, although a fence had to be built to keep it from roaming. It was obvious that the animal was lonesome, so a mate was obtained. The two lived in the pond for over ten years—each growing to over six feet in length.

In 1926, one of the other lakes was enlarged and built into the big, outdoor, hot-water swimming pool that is now one of the major attractions in Ouray. Thousands of people enjoy the pool in the summertime, but many more are learning what a relaxing experience it can be to swim or soak on winter days and evenings.

So now, a hundred years since the first tourists began to arrive in Ouray, visitors still continue to come, in greater and greater numbers, although the means of getting to the quaint little town have completely changed. No more is heard the rattle of the Concord coach, drawn by six powerful horses, as it pulls up in front of one of the hotels; no more is heard the musical tones of the whistle, the clanging of the bell, and the chuggity-chug of the train as it comes charging up the valley at twenty miles per hour; no more the "soft, soothing voices" of the wagon

❧ *From the time of the building of the large swimming pool in Ouray until the floods of 1929, tent-top cabanas were used as changing rooms. After the restoration of the pool in the spring of 1930, the first bathhouse was built. (Marvin and Ruth Gregory)*

drivers, the mule skinners, and the burro punchers as they speak gentle, affectionate words of encouragement to the tired little beasts. Any of the methods of travel which a hundred years ago were thought of as convenient, even luxurious, would today be considered too inefficient and disagreeable, if not actually painful!

Railroad spikes and burro shoes are now ardently sought by collectors. The miners' wagon roads into the mountains have become a principal attraction to thousands of four-wheel-drive enthusiasts who descend on the town every summer. A favorite winter pastime is ice climbing. Enthusiasts proclaim that the constant freezing and thawing in the Ouray area makes this some of the best climbing in the world!

And people come here just for the scenery. Cascade Falls is visible high above the town to the northeast; the water seemingly bursts forth from half way up the solid cliffs, shooting into space to finish as a veil of spray. A short hike ends at the waterfall (or actually behind it if one is daring enough). At the opposite end of town from the swimming pool is Box Canyon Falls, which has been a popular landmark since Ouray's founding. Here, the waters of Canyon Creek for almost two million years have sculptured a twisting, narrow, 215-foot-deep canyon, creating a never-ending roar that shakes the earth. In the 1890s, the local power company blasted a trail into the interior of the canyon to accommodate a pipeline to its hydroelectric plant, a route visitors immediately started using and still do, although the water line is gone. A steep upper trail leads to the High Bridge, where one can look directly down into the canyon.

Currently, there seems to be a trend toward perpetuating the architectural charm of the 1880s in the new buildings being constructed in Ouray. To the same end, a great deal of restoration has been done on some of the older buildings, many of which had previously lost much of their charm because of additions or remodeling. Or perhaps they had fallen victim of a period in the 1930s and 1940s when "old-fashioned" was unpopular and efforts were made either to remove or to conceal what was considered superfluous ornamentation or "ginger-bread."

It is entirely fitting that the town of Ouray should bear the name of the great Chief of the Tabeguache Utes, upon whose former domain it was built. Ouray was a ferocious fighter who rose to power within the Tabeguache group and was later appointed by the United States to become the first overall chief of the Ute Indians. He married Chipeta, who eventually became as well known and respected as Ouray.

It was Chief Ouray who, with uncanny wisdom and force of personality, for years prevented bloodshed between his people and the white men. He has often been called the "friend of the white man," which is perhaps unfair to him. He had the welfare of his own people very much at heart at all times. Skilled diplomat that he was, he was wise enough to realize that any armed conflict between his people and the white men would surely result in complete, final extermination of the Utes. Although they were robbed of much of their lands and banished to where the white man would never have tried to live, Ouray did keep his people from entering into a full-scale war in which they would have certainly perished. By skillful negotiations, the Utes stayed on their land for a decade after most Indians had been removed to Oklahoma Indian Territory. Throughout history, many men of greatness have received, posthumously, the honor due them. Chief Ouray, however, lived not only to experience the respect accorded him by white men, but to visit, on several occasions, a town named in his honor!

EPILOGUE

While the focus of this book has been the Million Dollar Highway, it has also had several other purposes: to provoke the natural spirit of adventure, to stimulate curiosity, to inspire an even greater love for the Creator's handiwork, and to fulfill a desire for accurate knowledge of the geology of the mountains and the history of some of the places along the route.

The Million Dollar Highway runs north and south through the heart of some of the most inspiring country in North America. There is no east-west thoroughfare across the San Juan Mountains, only old wagon roads and packtrails, a few of which may be traveled nowadays by four-wheel-drive vehicles. It has been most difficult for us to refrain from describing remote terrain accessible only by some of the trails that diverge from the Million Dollar Highway; there are so many paths to follow and so many places to go!

The soul and spirit of the San Juans is elusive: hundreds of books have been written and thousands of photographs taken with the disappointing result that, somehow, they always seem to fall a little short of capturing the true essence of the area. The San Juan country is a land in which the most delicate beauty and the most horrible hazards exist side by side. It is a land that holds tightly to its past yet realizes that it has a grand future. The scenery is so magnificent that it is bound to attract millions of visitors in the future, but the multitudes who come to enjoy its peace, tranquility, and great natural beauty may, by their very presence, be the ones to destroy it.

Perhaps it is appropriate to add poetry to the attempts of narrative writers and photographers to convey the ineffable qualities of these mountains—such as that articulated by Alfred Castner King, the poet of the San Juans. King was blinded in 1900 by an explosion in the Bachelor Mine near Ouray. He later wrote of the San Juans as he remembered them and as perhaps no one else has written before or since:

AN IDYLL

I love to sit by the waterfall,
    And list to its laughing story,
As it fearlessly leaps o'er the rocky wall,
    From the mountain peaks stern and
hoary;
Or watch the spray as the colors play,
    When the glorious sunlight kisses,
And tints confuse into rainbow hues
    To embellish the wild abysses.

I love the rose and the columbine,
    Whose delicate beauty pleases;
I love the breath of the fragrant pine,
    As it floats on the morning breezes;
I love the sound from the depths profound,
    When the Thunder-God is bringing
His crystal showers, to the tinted flowers,
    In their sweet profusion springing.

I love the lake in the mountain's lap;
    Without a flaw or error
Recording the clouds, which the
peaks enwrap,
    And the trees, as a crystal mirror;
The wild delights of the mountain heights
    Thrill my breast with a keen devotion,
As songbirds love the blue arch above,
    Or the mariner loves the ocean.

SUGGESTED READING

The whole picture of history is like a giant jigsaw puzzle made up of many pieces that may be found in different places. To locate some of the more important segments that compose the San Juans, we recommend the following books.

Early-day or primary sources must include *Crofutt's Grip-Sack Guide of Colorado - 1885* (reprinted by Johnson Books), which is a very accurate and informative tour guide. We also recommend Sidney Jocknick's *Early Days on the Western Slope of Colorado* (reprinted by the Rio Grande Press), one of the few factual and dependable firsthand accounts of the times immediately preceding and following the white man's mass arrival in the 1870s. The Rev. James J. Gibbons wrote an exciting and amusing account of his life, work, and extensive travels in the 1890s, entitled *In the San Juans* (reprinted by St. Patrick's Parish). Another pioneer preacher was the Rev. George A. Darley, who wrote *Pioneering in the San Juans* (reprinted by the Community Presbyterian Church of Lake City, Colorado). Harriet Fish Backus presents a woman's view of life in the area in her book, *Tomboy Bride* (Pruett Press).

Later accounts of life in the San Juans include: David Lavender's *One Man's West* (Doubleday-Duran), which relates the story of his life at the Camp Bird Mine during the Depression. Mr. Lavender also wrote *Red Mountain* (Popular Library)—which is technically a novel, but based on history—and many other books on the history of Colorado and the West. The Sarah Platt Decker Chapter of the N.S.D.A.R. has published *Pioneers of the San Juan Country* (Outwest Printing), a collection of stories, interviews, and memories of many of the old-timers in the Silverton and Animas Valley area. Louis Wyman has recorded his recollections of the early twentieth century in Silverton in a book entitled *Snow Flakes and Quartz* (San Juan County Book Co.). Evalyn Walsh McLean's *Father Struck It Rich* (Little, Brown & Co.) describes her life in Ouray and at the Camp Bird Mine at the turn of the century.

Books about railroads in the San Juans include the Colorado Rail Annuals, Numbers 9, 11, and 14 (Colorado Railroad Museum), which contain articles about Ouray and the Rio Grande Southern, but which include much more than the history of the railroads themselves. *The Rainbow Route* by Robert E. Sloan and Carl A. Skowronski (Sundance Limited) is a complete history of the Red Mountain-Silverton-Animas Forks area and is well researched and dependable, with many beautiful photographs. Doris Osterwald wrote *Cinders and Smoke* (United Printing and Publishing Co.), an excellent mile-by-mile guide to the Durango-to-Silverton narrow-gauge railroad trip. *Three Little Lines* (L.A. "Johnny" Johnson) by Josie Moore Crum is the story of the three short, independent railroad lines which originated in Silverton.

Freighting in the San Juans is well covered by Dorothy and Frances Wood in their book, *I Hauled These Mountains In Here* (The Caxton Printers). The authors did a good job of recording the story of David Wood, their father and the owner of the largest freight wagon outfit in the state of Colorado. Michael Kaplan has provided a thorough account of the life of Colorado's most famous toll road builder and of railroad building in general in *Otto Mears—Paradoxi-*

cal *Pathfinder* (San Juan County Book Co.).

The geology of the San Juans is well told by Thomas (Mel) Griffiths in his book, *San Juan Country* (Pruett Publishing Co.). Professor Griffiths is a mountain climber, writer, and photographer with a profound love and knowledge of the evolution and history of the area. An earlier geological tour of the region was presented in 1907 by T.A. Rickard in *Across the San Juan Mountains* (republished by the Bear Creek Publishing Company). Betsy R. and Richard L. Armstrong have coauthored excellent books about snow and avalanches in the San Juans, including *Avalanche Hazard in Ouray County, Colorado* and *A History of Avalanche Hazard in San Juan County, Colorado* (both published by the Institute of Arctic and Alpine Research, University of Colorado).

Books on the Ute Indians include a very fair, unbiased account called *People of the Shining Mountains* (Pruett Publishing Co.), by Charles S. Marsh, and *Ouray - Chief of the Utes* (Wayfinder Press), by P. David Smith. The latter is a history of the Utes in Colorado as well as a biography of the famous Ute chief.

Among the best known of contemporary histories of the area is Muriel Sibell Wolle's *Stampede to Timberline* (Swallow Press) and a later, updated version called *Timberline Tailings* (Swallow Press). Wilson Rockwell has written many books about the San Juans, including *Memoirs of a Lawman, Uncompahgre Country, The Utes, a Forgotten People,* and *New Frontiers* (all published by Sage Books). *A Land Alone* (Pruett Publishing Co.) is a recent comprehensive history of western Colorado by Duane A. Smith and Duane Vandenbusche. Professor Smith has also written *Rocky Mountain Boom Town - A History of Durango* (University of New Mexico Press), *Song of the Hammer and Drill* (CSM Press), and *Colorado Mining* (University of New Mexico Press). All are good, scholarly, and interesting histories. Jack Benham has published several brief histories, including *Ouray* and *Silverton* (both from Bear Creek Publishing Co.). Doris Gregory has written what one might call bits and pieces of Ouray history, including *Box Canyon, The Wright Opera House,* and *Era of Bars & Brothels* (all from Cascade Publishing Co.). Last but not least, Marvin Gregory and P. David Smith have also written *Mountain Mysteries - The Ouray Odyssey* (Wayfinder Press), which is a historical tour guide describing many of the ghost towns, jeep trails, mining tours, and roads in a large part of the San Juans.

The Authors

P. David Smith and Marvin Gregory, "Ourayites" who share a love of history as well as a fondness for southwestern Colorado, have brought their individual perspectives together again, this time to give us a wonderful look at Colorado's most scenic highway. They were coauthors of the very popular book, *Mountain Mysteries–The Ouray Odyssey*, and Mr. Smith has also written *Ouray–Chief of the Utes.*

The Photographer

Kathleen Norris Cook, whose color photographs capture the spirit and beauty of the highway, has received considerable recognition. Her work has been published by Arizona Highways, Citicorp, Eastman Kodak, The National Geographic Society, the National Park Service, the Sierra Club, and VISA USA. She makes her home in Ouray several months of the year.